The Dark and Grey Thoughts Of Life

By

Kevin Hitesman

Case ID: 1-13570200518

Paper Back ISBN: 978-1-304-43055-7
Hardcover ISBN: 978-1-304-42996-4

Dedication

I want this to be dedicated to brother, David who died in 1990 at the age of 11.

My name is Kevin Hitesman I am 41 years old.
I'm originally am from Idaho I was born in a small town known as Twin falls, Id in the magic valley Hospital. I was raised in a small town called Glennsferry, ID and a small city Boise ID. I don't know a lot about my childhood from when I was an infant to 4 years of age. What I do know is I was left in a crib up to two years of age and when I was six months old I was malnourished and a week away from dying as a baby.
There are a lot of lies in my life that I have been told I will never know the truth.
I know there was a lot of abuse between my parents and towards my brothers and sisters and I; I have always loved to write. I been writing since I was in High School and even when I graduated High School in 2001. I grew up in an abusive broken home as well as witnessed my brother's death on December 11th 1990, I was at a very young age. One week later my dad and my oldest sister by five years get into a heated fight and all's I know is that

my sister had to leave the house for good. Two weeks later my Dad, up and leaves without telling any of us. I remember not seeing my dad all day, so I walk down the ally to my grandparents. They lived two houses down from where we lived from the backyard where the ally is. I had asked if they had seen my dad, they said "no we have not seen him all day". They decided to have all three of us to live with them. So it was my older brother, my sister and I. After living with my grandparents for four years my sister and I were forced to move back in with my dad. My sister who is a year older than I am. We don't get along at all there is no love between us. From there is where my school years would haunt me, and be very disappointed to me and to sec that I was a failure and no kids or teachers would deal with me or tolerate me for nothing. I was made fun of, bullied humiliated was taught just to do easy work and move on. Not even football or sport coaches would help me when I asked for help to understand to get better I was ignored and no one wanted to go out of their way to help me. Not even to get better when I had asked for help. Teachers ignored me as much as they could, teachers and bullies made my school years to become nightmares. When I stood up for myself I was the one who got into trouble not even my friends stood up for me in fact they scorned me for standing up for myself. So needless to say, I have tried to go back to college it was a failure. I'm always working and needing to pay my bills. From my family to very early years in elementary school, middle school, I had always had to take special Ed classed because of my learning disability that I had, I was told that I was not to going to amount to much or anything in my life. Teachers did not want to deal with me or my ADD and I got passed on from one grade to another. I did try my best to be a good student but it took me longer too understand the material and I even had teachers call me dumb and stupid while rolling their eyes when I tried to participate. I got bullied a lot and no one stood up for me so I had to stand up for myself cause I had not one person in my corner. I also had family members treat me like I was a ghost and I was not there in existence. I had family tell me I was dumb as well and left me out. I was always left behind even with my friends I was left on the outside looking in being made fun of all the time. People did not know how to deal with me cause I did not have the social skills I needed due to my up bringing. I was left in a crib being Malnourished and a week away from dying while being left abandoned. My brother committed suicide at the age of 11 in 1990 I was 6 at that time. My life has always been hard and tough, always an outcast and when I have tried to learn or be with friends I was a cast away. I remember being in a youth group and I wanted to sing I stood up there in front of the church with other kids we started to sing and everybody started to Laugh and make fun of me and tore me down hard. It broke me as a kid that is how my life has always been. Now I'm 41 and have my own family and I work two full time jobs I write. And do music. I am License Nursing Assistant and have been for a number of years it's really the only thing I'm good at in life. I have worked for Hospital systems and many different nursing homes I have my own business and I have a song out on YouTube and Spotify called Get a Grip by me or CUSTOMCUTSTUDIOES. No one believed in me that I would make as far as I have in my life or where I am at. I gave God the praise and glory for bringing me this far. My teenage years were hard and full of hard lessons. Tried to fit in but could not while I was living with my dad we were on government assistance and used my social security paychecks to pay the bills instead of working. We got food stamps, section 8 housing and medical benefits while I was on Social security. We were very poor. Grew up in the Mormon church so we also used the Mormon store to buy groceries as well it's important to know im not Mormon any more. My dad let everybody raise me but himself. There was no fishing trips or camping or drives the excuse was we have no money to do anything. I vowed when I became a parent we would do those things. I am working all the time to make ends meet. I work 6 days a week 12 hour shifts.

I try to make time for my kids but it's hard.

I thank God for the ability to write, it allows me to express myself freely of any judgement or bigotry of any kind. It allows me to express my emotions that I cannot tell anybody else, chains are broken when I write. It allows me to be me just simply who I am. That's why I made this book cause it helps me express my anguish my misery my doubts my selfness, my worries my depression I am free when I write. So, thank you.

PRAISE BE TO GOD for bringing me this far in my life he has raised me up and held mc close. I may have had to learn very hard lessons and I choose to do things in my life when I walked away from God but even in those times he let me know he was near all the time. My point to all of this my life has been very hard, very abusive up bringing in a broken home believing in what others have told me I would be or what I couldn't be. I was told I couldn't be a sales person or a people person I would always live at home with someone. I just got tired of listing to other people make decisions and choices for me or talk me into things I did not want to do. So, this is me breaking free.

Table of Contents

Chapter: 1

UNBREAKABLE CHAINS:

I may not be rich,
I may not be muscular,
I may not be smart or whitty,
But I work for those who are with me.
For family I'll do anything for,
For the ones I deeply LOVE and CARE ABOUT.
Our Souls are one our spirits touch one another you are mine and I am yours.
The door is open as we walk through together hand in hand with the bond of one that is unmatched and never changing.
Your one string has become three strings that is unbreakable.
It's an uphill battle but will you fight with me?
Will you fight for me? And stand side by side with me? I will hold you as you become enthralled into me as our hearts beat as one core. Give into me as I have Given

into you for no longer is the fight a struggle but submerging into the strength of the Love.

That is in me that is in you I can no Longer bear but only to give into…

IT TAKES EVERYTHING YOU'VE GOT:

It takes everything you've got,
You give everything you've got,
Leave everything you have,
It takes time to Master the thing you want.
No regrets for the thing you've missed no matter how many times you have been dissed.
Give everything you've got,
Give everything you've have,
Don't leave anything behind.
Been in it too long it's time for a change.
Tired of taking a backseat, tried to raise my voice but it gets drowned in the noise.
Life has tried to defeat me, beat me, so now I'm running for my life
Escaping the pain setting a new course to be free.
I Love to fight cause that's part of the struggle figuring out where to land not caring what the man thinks.
The adrenaline is a drug I Love the feeling of the rush.

LIVING ON A D.I.M.E.

I can't live on a dime anymore.

So tired so weary I want to cry.

I'm so worn down I walk a lonely road,

in my town.

I'm in a dark place hiding in a dark corner.

My memory fading away,

Entering the unknown gate that what is to become of my fate.

I have no friends to let me know so now I have to go on my own.

I want to tell my story but I don't know how.......

BROTHER LYING STILL:

I can't forget what I have seen while I walked home from the church on that crisp evening night as my heart pounded as I took flight.

Walked in the front door only to see my brother lying still.

As I stood in the front door, trembling, my feet couldn't move from the floor, and I saw you lay still on the stretcher being blue and purple; as your last breath was taken away from being strung up.

No I can't forget, what I have seen,

I can remember that day like it was yesterday.

How long ago you were taken away.

I have tried to carry on for these many years.

Spent countless time crying out these tears.

Life has been long and hard for so many years since the day you died. I never forget that day when I saw you lay still while your heart stopped.

I didn’t shed a tear I really couldn’t understand what happened at the time when I was young but I continued to live in fear each and every day. when I took a step,
I was scared. I wish you were near so I could hear your advice but you're in heaven for over thirty years.
I remember the day like it was yesterday.
How long ago you were taken away.
Now I know your angel up in heaven watching down over me.
I remember that day like it was yesterday how long ago you were taken away.

SEXUAL SUBMISSION:

Allow the mind to go into a state of erotic stimulating arousal as your sexual desire becomes more stronger with every thought, with every, movement of my touch as my voice paralyzes you as, you are helpless a bit only able to follow commands from hearing my voice. Your body is flooded with your juices just by my presence as I begin to touch you in ways that you have never been touched before. It’s different it means something more than you realize. The sensation of sexual erotic play, you submerge yourself into a subconscious that you presently come into my will my sexual loving woman. The uncontrollable the sexual demons coming out is unbearable of not getting enough. As we are away it's that drive that keeps bringing you back into my world.

The sight of whom I am in your eyes

The sound of my voice with the base in the tone that gets your mind going as it trickles down to your pussy, as you start to get wet uncontrollably.

The smell of my body that's sets your sexual ecstasy desire off as your body tingles with every movement all your muscles start to tighten up as your pussy is wet down to your ass. As you think of me your sexual desire gets stronger and stronger as I am on your mind with every step and every move you make. You have no choice but to surrender it unto me.

Deceit:

Deceit lays in bed with lies.

All the demons have eyes.

My life has been in pain.

My heart has been in suffering.

My environment has let me learn to be angry.

There is no justification in the room of lies.

At the end I have no one to say by too;

There are countless endless ties,

This life is shortly lived here I am running out of time.

What does this life have a meaning of?

I am the only one that is so far away.

MUSIC IS THE SOUL:

The beats never stop music is the soul, we bring it to the ground while your ear listens to the sounds. Until you come around it's always popping rocking, non-stopping and the beats keep on thumping. As you thrash around it gets your heart pumping. Set your soul free let your spirit arise, let your mind be surprised come with me and dance with me.

LURKING INSIDE:

I know what lurks inside you the very thing that is wanting to wake up but yet you been ignoring it. Close your eyes, free your mind let go of control; share your mind share your body. Share your spirit see your deepest, sexual fantasy let us bring them out to play. Let your fantasy be dominated in the hands of someone you trust and let's dig deep into your subconscious, let's explore your sexual desirable nature. LET GO BE FREE, LET GO BE FREE, LET GO BE FREE. Allow the sexual heavy rage burst out into super organic sensation like you have never felt before.

Let your body be controlled let your pussy be wet and glistening as your body starts to spams and all control is lost except to who dominating you as you easily submit. At the moment you choose to submit is the moment you have trusted me into making a sexual organic erotic ecstasy pleasure of enjoying every inch every hole every touch of your body and mind. Mind play is weakening you into my bosom as you are being toyed with as your pussy seeks pleasure you look at me with desperate eyes as a puppy looking at her master. Come and enjoy the pleasure of the company that I present. Let your world unfold into the grasp of my bosom let your eroticism come to a mountain of volcanic ecstasy of organic eruption that makes you be brought down to your knees as I play with you as I take you into a whole another world that you have never been too.

RUBBING BODY:

Each time you take a step, every movement you make, you think of me; as you think of me more and more as I become heavy in your mind so does your pussy get wet and keeps getting wetter. Your nipples get harder as you gulp your saliva down your throat. The racing you feel inside you is your heart beating harder and faster you start to curl your lips just the mere thought of me touching you rubbing you with my hand as your body is being caressed. Each time you sit down or stand up you feel the gushing wetness come down your legs as your mind wonders. At this point it is uncontrollable until you're in my presence as your body melts into mine. Your lips are soft and moist to kiss as my hands reaches on each side of you kissing you hard. My hands rubbing your back, down to your ass rubbing your panties up against you with a gentle touch as you go crazy as your already wet. Your mind already into mine as your eyes tell me to take you.

You are deep in trance to me. Your body melts into mine as you are willing to give yourself up to me with no hesitation. Our spirits merges together that intertwines in this parallel universe under the heavens. You are hypnotize into my life as you become submissive unto me.

PUNCHING BAG:

Burning, boiling; hell fire hot I have had no hope in life without a pot to piss in.

Growing up with abandonment issues

not fitting in socially missing all the cues.

Being by myself with hardly any kids to talk,

too which was only a few.

They said they were my friends only to realize I was their punchline at the end of the joke to be talked about behind my back.

Always been the punching bag. My own family wanting nothing to do with me I was tossed away like I was a piece of trash left as six-month-old not being fed on the brink of death. Been left alone with no one to hug onto or to tell my problems too no parents around.

Been left for dead counted out before my life had even begun.

Had dreams but I was told by everyone I'm no good for nothing.

Even teachers in school shoved me in the corner and left to be forgotten about.

Tired of taking a backseat tried to raise my voice but it gets drowned in the noise.

life has tried to defeat me, beat me so now I'm running for my life escaping the pain setting a new course to be free.

I Love to fight cause that's part of the struggle figuring out where to land not caring what the man thinks.

The adrenaline is a drug I Love the feeling of the rush.

Heart Attack:

I'm running away like I'm having a heart attack, we used to look up at the stars and used to dream, big dreams then the real world came crashing down on us. Not looking up, not knowing what hit us. Going down the road spinning in a whirlpool who's going to save us now? Oh I think the lights are out I see the stars diminishing from my eyesight. Someone cut the strings I'm falling, I feel like I'm on fire look around but the desires gone out of my soul what to do now? What to make sense of it all? There is nothing more in life then a reassuring a warm welcome to hold me up, to help me, keep my head up instead of dipping down losing all control because there nothing more sinister than losing your own soul to the hate of this world.

SONG:

(Verse 1)

In the burrow of struggle, where defeat meets your gaze,
Hold on tight, take courage, as the light guides your ways.
Don't surrender, don't give in, though you've lost your might,
Keep fighting through the night, the light's your beacon,
bright.

(Chorus)

I'll be here for you, a shoulder to lean on,
No need to swim in confusion, the pond is all gone.
With the light on for you, don't give up the fight,
Keep pushing through the darkness, embrace the
guiding light.

(Verse 2)

In this battle of shadows, where doubt
tries to creep,
Stand tall, stay resolute, let the promises you keep.

If your strength falters, if your spirit's feeling worn,
Remember, through the night, a new day is born.

(Chorus)
I'll be here for you, a harbor in the storm,
No need to navigate alone, I'll keep you warm.
With the light on for you, don't give in to despair,
We'll conquer the challenges, a duo beyond compares.

(Bridge)
When the world seems cold, and the road feels long,
Lean on my support, let our solidarity be
strong.
Together we'll weather whatever trials may come,
Under the gleaming light, a journey we've begun.

(Chorus)
I'll be here for you, a constant, steadfast friend,
In the symphony of life, our harmonies blend.
With the light on for you, don't let hope fade away,

Keep dancing through the darkness, a brighter dawns on its way.

(Outro)
So, don't give up, don't give in, our story's far from through,
In this shared adventure, the light's forever on for you.

Chapter 2

LIVING ON A DIME Song Version:

I can't live on a dime anymore,

So tired so weary I want to cry,

I'm so worn down I walk a lonely road.

in my town.

I'm in a dark place hiding in a dark corner.

My memory fading away,

Entering the unknown gate that what is to become of my fate.

I have no friends to let me know so now I have to go on my own.

I want to tell my story but I don't know how.

LEFT BLACK & BLUE

The roads I have always been on has always been on fire always walking through the burning flames no matter how hard I worked, no matter how hard I've tried. I have lost after loss its my truth, their lie. Whoever cared? Whoever Loved? I was left fighting for my life never dreamed, never shared only just to keep fighting to survive just for the day. Left abandoned, left with bruises and scars torn apart never had a start.

I need a cold hard stiff drink I have no strings to pull don't even know how much more I can hold life has been one big tragedy for me but I have no one to plea, too.

Brown Liquor cold boots nobody but you and me. Left alone I was hurt no pipeline to go to. Always been on my own always been cold, always been on the outside never accepted for who I am, living a life full of regret. Always dark, always troubled always working for short change. All's I do is live in pain, the past is constantly eating at me I try to move on and live for my kids but it comes and drags me back down into that hole. My life is a sad song living on these back roads. Been tore up cuts' n bruises skin torn off, all my life been left black and blue.

APPREHENSION:

Apprehension no Appreciation I'm the only one in my association the calibration is in my head without no celebration. Distraught miss-taught with no coalition runnin' on a mission only to get into a collision. Life has not gone my way but I've worked hard, never given up, never playing with a full hand but I've step up to the challenge I'm still here, I'm still standing no one given me a hand I rock my words in my head. Overwhelmed I'm into deep stepping on the edge of the helm I have lost so much in my life that I forgot what is to win. I hear my voice cry out save me from myself as my feet slip off the edge. It's time, it is finally happening; I am falling to the end as my heart is pounding. I hear the sound to the ending of my demise, I'm weeping in vein as blood pours out my chest.

NOT GIVING UP:

When I'm going to get mine, I promise you; you going to quit on a dime this time around is different.

I'm wakin' up going into work I'm workin' for a living I give them a yes as they have me a no, I dig deep to reassure myself but it's still the same.

What is right? what is wrong? Why is the world spinning upside down? Been the odd one out, looking from the outside in, changes are here changes are not going anywhere. Changes are hard never ending the constant struggle will be, but out comes strength.

Through the pain, pain makes you have the fears, pain makes you face your fears it opens your eyes when you can't see. Speak life and see it rain down on you. This life is toxic no this ain't no can of tonic life has taken shots in parody hit it in, hit it out, I have been drowned while being broken. Learned how to get caught up. Crash and burn is what we do. We also learn to live with scars, at night we are to look up at the stars. We know a better day will be brighter.

REMEMBER THE OLD DAYS:

Remember the old days when I was written off in people's lives? But I was no phase to others I was just in a small lonely place. Just slightly in somewhat good graces even then I was my own man runin' down other people just to be liked. But I was in a box trying to be a shape shifter, finally I broke free only to be me. I would hit the ceiling only to fall hard on my face but had no choice but to get back up and stay in the same place to be broken. Humble but also strong. Had no money for a gold chain, struggling, begging being poor, felt like everything was raining down on me. No way, no chance but I had not refused to give up, being filled by desire determined to make it no matter the cost. No one raised me up in the kitchen so I was my own boss. While others put me in categories. I'm just not another story,
You get in my way I'll pick up a knife carve your eyes out. Red eyes seeing nothing but red I'm ready for a fight, I'm still standing here.

No, I won't go till my last breath is done.

All’s you see left is smoke from the gun this life has meant for me not to have any fun.

I'm not trying to hide myself from anyone or anything I just don't feel free or feel anything as a man. Your excepted to be strong and hold it together but underneath it all I crumble and fall.

I'm trying to live my life as free as I can but circumstances keep me hindered.

Tired of leaning on my own.

SWEET SOUND:

Please let me hear your heart beat,

To my ears is a melody a sweet sound to my soul.

A soothing sweet memory to ease the pain away.

There is nothing else to gain.

So please let me hear your heart beat as it is a sweet

melody to my ears, that's a sweet sweet sound to my soul.

The loneliness goes away and I know that I've been found

to share with some one who is always around.

For the darkness to go away, ohh, we paved our own way

so let's keep believing that it never fades away.

SLAVES TO SELFISHNESS:

Temperament is one that is a dangerous thing that we wear as our crowns. That we wear that is unseen. It tells our stories whether or not people want to hear. The truth that is told shall not be and the non-truth shall be heard when it is a farce with a fake cry of men. The helping of one another is no more but only selfish ambition to those whom are for only themselves. We are slaves to selfishness with no hope of light that guides us. True Love is very rare now.

In shadows cast by unseen crowns we bear,
Our temperaments, dangerous tales declare.
Stories whispered, whether sought or shunned,
Truth veiled, in silence or non-truth spun. A farce adorned with a fake cry of men, Selfish ambitions prevail, compassion's end. No helping hands, just egos in pursuit,
We've become slaves to selfishness, lost in the brute.
Yet, in this darkness, a faint hope ignites, Guided not by self, but by love's pure lights.

In rare moments, love's genuine glare,
Breaks through the gloom, a solace so rare.

LONER:

I'm a loner no matter where I have been?

I'm an outcast no matter whom I'm with?

Always seems that I'm alone as I roam.

What's the cause of my loneliness that everyone abandoned me? Only so much hurt being ripped out of me. Playing my own character; in my own show of being absurd. Don't have a good bloodline, there is something away don't know what I'm missing been gone for so long I am astray in the streets. It doesn't matter how much I pray. I have nothing to say everything is in the wind tears wiped away. My being at war tearing conflict don't know what to do any more. Just make me into a war machine, war is ugly, war is pain, war is death, nobody wants me this black Sunday in a mass of witches at black masses. I try to hang on but only to be revered by other people having only to hold onto hate the only shield I can wield is the one full of rage, vengeance and hate. I've been crucified for who I am to be never could I really never trust anyone.

RUN, FEAR, RAGE:

I run with fear, I play with rage, while hate consumes me one thing remains. She stays with me no matter what. I dance in fires, doesn't matter how many times I have been burned; she is always right there by my side defending my horrible nature. She has changed me even though I have been down in despair. My body is my punching bag, blood running down my cheek as I abuse myself with my fist striking flesh of my own body as I have grown tolerant to self abuse. I have come over to the darkness away from the light.

So come close to me and close your eyes as you feel my breath upon your face as my eyes gazes at your beautifulness let your head rest upon my breath of my chest.

HEADSPACE:

POEM:

I'm not in the right headspace; I seem to be out of control. In the midst of problematic life, no solutions to behold as frustrating as it is its seems like I've lost grip on my reality. I promised myself I would have a better life than when I was a kid now, I reflect on where it wrong.
I pray that I can change today. But I am only a thread hair away from falling apart. I think about jumping off a roof top to end it all but then where would I be what would life look like for them. Where is there a glimmer of hope?

SONG:

(Verse 1)
In the shadows of my mind, lost and out of control,
A life so problematic, solutions hard to hold.
Frustration gripping tight, reality slips away,
Promised myself a better life, but I'm lost in disarray.

(Pre-Chorus)

I reflect on where it went wrong,
A childhood dream, now a distant song.
Praying for change, today's the day,
But hanging by a thread, just a hair away.

(Chorus)

I won't jump off that rooftop, no,
For there's more to life, I need to know.
A glimmer of hope, somewhere it lies,
In the depths of despair, a chance to rise.

(Verse 2)

I'm wrestling with demons, memories of the past,
A promise broken; shadows cast.
Yet, deep within, a desire to be free,
To rewrite the script, of my destiny.

(Bridge)

Life’s a puzzle, pieces scattered wide,
I search for hope, with arms open wide.
The rooftop’s tempting, but I resist,
For in the struggle, I may find bliss.

(Chorus)

I won’t jump off that rooftop, no,
For there’s more to life, I need to know.
A glimmer of hope, somewhere it lies,
In the depths of despair, a chance to rise.

(Outro)

Though the journey’s tough, and the path is steep hold on to hope do not let it seep. Life is a melody with highs, lows in a symphony of survival our story grows.

FRIENDS FROM THE OTHER SIDE:

Here I am in land of opportunity on my feet taking a stand but here I come to stir the pot, while I start the controversy how is this going around without me? Let me talk to my friends from the other side.

Here I am to start the cause please sit no need for applause its only me but not everyone can see how much trouble I get blamed for, let's not drag this into court, so my dear sweet souls allow me to talk to my friends from the other side.

You look familiar please don't pull that trigger you don't remember seeing each other? I tried to tell to you but you just did not want to listen you were to stay away now let me call on my friends from the other side oh please don't beg. Because here are my friends from the other side.

SONG TO THE POEM

(Verse 1)

In the land of opportunity, I stand tall,

Taking a stand, ready to give my all.

Stirring the pot, starting controversy,

Wondering why it goes on without me.

(Chorus)

Here I am, starting a cause,

No need for applause, just my own flaws.

Not everyone sees the trouble I bear,

Let's not drag this into a courtroom affair.

(Verse 2)

You look familiar, don't pull that trigger,

Do you recall, our paths crossed, remember?

Tried to warn you, but you wouldn't listen,

You were supposed to stay away, now it's a mission.

(Pre-Chorus)

Let me call on my friends from the other side,
Oh, please don't beg, no need to hide.

(Chorus)

Here I am, starting a cause,
No need for applause, just my own flaws.
Not everyone sees the trouble I bear,
Let's not drag this into a courtroom affair.

(Bridge)

In the rhythm of the night, a tale unfolds,
A story of warnings, but the tale's been told.
Caught in the crossfire, memories linger,
A plea for understanding, as emotions trigger.

(Verse 3)

So here I am, in the midst of the storm,
Trying to make sense, finding a norm.

Friends from the other side, they lend a hand,
But please don't beg, in this complex land.

(Chorus)
Here I am, starting a cause,
No need for applause, just my own flaws.
Not everyone sees the trouble I bear,
Let's not drag this into a courtroom affair.

(Outro)
As the curtain falls, and the echoes fade,
In the heart of controversy, a choice is made.
Listen closely, and you might find,
The harmony within the chaos, intertwined.

BAD INTENTIONS:

Hey how's it going?

It's going very well?

Just thinking; talking to my demon friends on the other side.

My eyes see far and wide,

It's nice to know your intention.

Oh, I forgot to mention how crazy I can be the reason is it sets me free.

Don't have a very good attention.

(Verse 1)

Hey, how's it going?

It's going so well, can't you tell?

Thinking and talking, with my demons on the other side,

Eyes wide open, seeing far and wide.

(Chorus)

Nice to know your intention,

Forgot to mention, how crazy I can be,

The reason is clear, it sets me free.
No good attention, but that's me.

(Verse 2)
Lost in thoughts, a mind's ascension,
Demons whispering, their own dimension.
Crazy vibes, in my own convention,
Setting me free, no need for apprehension.

(Bridge)
Dancing with shadows, in the moonlight,
Embracing the madness, feeling so right.
Attention slips, like a fleeting night,
I'm the reason, my own guiding light.

(Chorus)
Nice to know your intention,
Forgot to mention, how crazy I can be,
The reason is clear, it sets me free.
No good attention, but that's me.

(Outro)

In the chaos, I find my peace,

With my demons, conversations cease.

Craziness is my release,

In this wild mind, were thoughts never, cease.

CAN'T HOLD IT TOGETHER:

I can't hold it together anymore.

Everything around me is falling apart,

I thought I could handle everything going on in my life.

But it seems I'm keep getting deeper in the hole and I'm unable to dig myself out.

Everything is spinning out of control,

My grip is slipping on the handle that I have; I don't have a hold of nothing that is tangible.

Everyone and everything are slipping away from me why I am left so cold and alone.

Why does nothing ever work out for me what's with me?

The scars just keep opening up the wounds never heal I'm about to burst from the inside of me.

(Verse 1)

I can't hold it together anymore

Everything around me is falling apart.

I thought I could handle everything in my life.

But it seems I'm keep getting deeper in the hole, can't find the light.

(Pre-Chorus)
Everything is spinning out of control
My grip is slipping, I'm losing my hold.

On everything that's tangible, I can't deny.
Everyone and everything are slipping away, I wonder why.

(Chorus)
Why am I left so cold and alone?
Why does nothing ever work out for me, what's wrong with my tone?
The scars just keep opening up, the wounds never heal
I'm about to burst from the inside, it's so hard to deal.

(Verse 2)
I search for answers in the darkest of nights.
Hoping for a sign, for a glimmer of light.
But it feels like I'm drowning in this sea of doubt.
The weight on my shoulders, I can't figure out.

(Pre-Chorus)
Everything is spinning out of control
My grip is slipping, I'm losing my hold.
On everything that's tangible, I can't deny.
Everyone and everything are slipping away, I wonder why.

(Chorus)
Why am I left so cold and alone?
Why does nothing ever work out for me, what's wrong with my tone?
The scars just keep opening up, the
Wounds never heal.
I'm about to burst from the inside, it's so hard to deal.

(Bridge)

But in the midst of this storm, I'll find my way.
I'll rise from the ashes, see a brighter day.
Though I've been broken and bruised, I'll still stand tall.
I'll mend the wounds, won't let my spirit fall.

(Chorus)

Why am I left so cold and alone?
Why does nothing ever work out for me, what's wrong with my tone?
The scars just keep opening up, the wounds never heal.
I'm about to burst from the inside, it's so hard to deal.

(Outro)

I'll fight through the darkness, find strength within.
I won't let this pain define where I've been.
I'll keep pushing forward, breaking these chains.
With hope in my heart, I'll ease all the pain.

WHISKY:

Overtime, you age just, right? There is no fight. You come to me with no end in sight and accept me for who I am so come to me, my good old friend that I call my good old whiskey and lead me home to let me roam.

Take away the pain and the loneliness As I put the blues on the radio know not where to go, I drank my good old whiskey that stays.

It's a sad song when my whiskey is all gone away. Thank you for the memories of the good old fight. And now I'm age, just right. Thank you for leading me to the end. As now I’m home with my good old friend that good old whiskey that taste just right.

Chapter 3:

Truth is hard to tell:

The truth is hard to tell; A lie is easily said. The truth is a lie that no one uses. I've always been misused so please tell me why? So come on, tell me what's on your mind? Why are you always so inclined to deny me a simple truth? You have taken, taken, taken, away from me the Innocence of what could be made. You made me an outcast, did not know any better to be livin the fast life. You gave me the power to give up. Taught me nothing but to be helpless, so I became strong and not useless, gave myself tools to use. I was made in pain, raised in suffering, and now I have the world to gain. I'm my own man, standing on my own two feet, I found a way out, I woke up out the nightmare. Created a life for myself to where I'm at now. So please tell me for God's Sake why is it so hard to speak. The truth is hard to tell. A lie is easily said. The truth is a line that no one uses I've always been misused so please tell me why?

LIFE'S A DRUG:

Life is a drug sipping on straight chemicals. Life is a rush wondering about. Only to get crushed life was once full of hope and dreams, but then everything came to a holstering scream. been up, been down, built new ground, but stepped out and sunk down. Silence is a drowning pool, your thoughts betray it's a tool to be used so let us listen to cues but hey at least I know I'm alive and have a soul. Life is a drug to keep me away from distant memories. Walk out to the edge it looks really good entices me to be its friend surviving the day taking it hour by hour.

(Verse 1)

Life's a drug, sipping on chemicals,
In this rush, wondering where it goes.
Full of hope and dreams, once it gleamed,
But it came crashing down in a holstering scream.

(Chorus)

Up and down, built new ground,
Stepped out, but then I sunk down.
Silence is a drowning pool,
Thoughts betray, it's a tool.
Listen to cues, in this game we play,
At least I know I'm alive, got a soul today.

(Verse 2)

Life's a drug, keeping distant memories away,
Walk to the edge, looks good, entices me to stay.
Surviving the day, taking it hour by hour,
In this dance with life, feeling its power.

(Bridge)

A symphony of highs and lows,
In this journey where life flows.
Echoes of dreams, now distant and far,
Yet, I stand, beneath the shooting star.

(Chorus)

Up and down, built new ground,
Stepped out, but then I sunk down.
Silence is a drowning pool,
Thoughts betray, it's a tool.
Listen to cues, in this game we play,
At least I know I'm alive, got a soul today.

(Outro)

Life's a drug, a complex melody,
In this world, finding my destiny.
Hour by hour, day by day,
In the rhythm of life, I find my way.

MORNING RHYTHMS:

Beat lying down, I’m beat waking up, I start over again as the night visit at the tail end.

As the morning starts to take over as my body bends, the sound of feet shuffling.
In the rhythm of defeat, a weary heart's retreat,
Lying down, each beat echoing the day's defeat.
Morning whispers, the night at its tail end,
A dance of resilience as darkness descends.

Waking up, a silent vow to begin anew,
As the night's visit fades, morning's cue.
Body bending, a silent surrender to the dawn,
The shuffle of feet, a symphony reborn.

In the quiet cadence, a tale unfolds,
Of cycles, relentless, as life unfolds.
A poetic journey, night to morn's embrace,
A resilient spirit in this rhythmic space.

VOICE LOST:

(Verse 1)

Tired of taking a backseat, voice lost in the noise,
Life tried to defeat me, but I'm escaping, making my choice.
Raising my voice, against the pain I've known,
Setting a new course, I'm breaking free, on my own.

(Chorus)

I love the fight, it's part of the struggle,
Not caring what they say, in this life's puzzle.
Adrenaline's my drug, feeling the rush,
Navigating through the chaos, breaking the hush.

(Verse 2)

Life tried to beat me down, but I won't
succumb,
Running for my life, a new journey begun.
Figuring where to land, in this wild ride,
Defying expectations, I'll let my spirit guide.

(Chorus)
I love the fight, it's part of the struggle,
Not caring what they say, in this life's puzzle.
Adrenaline's my drug, feeling the rush,
Navigating through the chaos, breaking the hush.

(Bridge)
Against the odds, I'll find my way,
A warrior's heart, won't lead astray.
The struggle shapes me, like an artist's brush,
In the canvas of life, I create my own hush.

(Verse 3)
I embrace the challenge, the thrill of the unknown,
Finding strength within, seeds of resilience sown.
No approval needed, from the judgmental gaze,
I dance with my shadows, through life's intricate maze.

(Chorus)

I love the fight, it's part of the struggle,
Not caring what they say, in this life's puzzle.
Adrenaline's my drug, feeling the rush,
Navigating through the chaos, breaking the hush.

(Outro)

So here I stand, not defined by the past, A melody of resilience, a song that will last. In the rhythm of life, I find my key, For in the struggle, I discover the real me.

HANGING ON CONNECTIONS:

You're a clown in a mask, excuse me while I get my surgical mask on. Been cut to deep, now it's my turn to do the cutting. I know I mental now I resent you. Been researching to find a way to take you out. I'm not by polar but I'm up, I'm down, been trying to find a recipe to help me but nothing seems to work other people tried to break me up. All's I have had is questions but all I have gotten in answers is silence. Backs have been against me, who turned on me? Why do I get left hanging? No education as I am disconnected. Who reaches out there to hear my messages? As I try to reconnect but yet everyone is running from me. This world tried to bury me six feet deep as a baby, as a child into my adulthood. Don't mind me as I become sonically where I am at, I am the pinnacle of my life everyone is plastic, plain, stupid and fake.

CONTEMPLATING DELUSIONAL:

I'm Contemplating, isolating, being delusional give me a path, supervision,

Contradiction how come you won't let me out? Never forget me no matter where I'm at. Know I have given it my all. I just have fallen I'm too far gone. My head is exploding my soul is on fire what the hell do you want from me? I'm implementing for my life but all the monsters around me had a knife and has cut me. Why are you trying to play me? I'm not breaking, my life is mine you better watch out cause I'm coming back with vengeance. I'm addicted to pain and suffering and you are twisted your freaking me out. Your soul is not welcomed here, be gone before I cut your eyes out. No surprises you can't do anything now come at me if you must. I'm letting you know you're going to get burned so come shout for me. I don't need you any more I'm separating myself from you, I'm not needed, going on my own way, I'll figure it out. Now that I own it, I need it, I can't live without it, why? Because I’m too far gone. No one near me, no one to hear me scream from the inside out, why? Because I’m too far gone for anyone to help me. I'm here but where? I’m too far gone. The rage is here but it is like a fire to the wind blowing everywhere, burning everything in its pathway because I am too far gone.

LOST TO ME DUE TO DARKNESS:

Lost to me due to time, been blind due to everything stolen from me; my life has been a crime been forgotten about counted out.

Shoved on the streets,

Due or die keep it simplified going to end up being magnified.

(I'm only a man living simply as I can. Never had a mamma to care, never had a daddy to understand Oh ohh don't ya know I'm living as simply as I can but know I am only a man).

I hope what I did for today makes a difference for tomorrow.

You ask a question but when I come back,

You are nowhere to be found.

Don't ya Know I'm just a man living to die.

Never learned myself how to love myself.

I'm only a man who will ever understand me of who I am?

At the end of the journey, I will meet you at the cross roads.

SONG: HEAVY HEART:

Each time you take a step, every movement you make, you think of me more and more as I become heavy in your mind.

So does your pussy as it gets super wet and keeps gushing out pussy juice as your nipples get harden as you spit all over your tits, as you gulp it down your throat. The racing you feel inside you as your heart is beating harder and faster. You start to curl your lip with just the mere thought of me racing through you, as you feel me touching you, rubbing you with my hand as your body is being caressed. Each time you sit down or stand up you feel the gushing juices wetness come down your legs as your mind wonders. At this point it is uncontrollable until you are in my presence as you melt into me. Your lips are soft and moist to kiss as my hands reaches on each side of you kissing you hard. My hands rubbing your back down to your ass rubbing your panties up against you with a gentle touch, a rough touch persuade as you get crazy with a very moisturizing dripping wet succulent soaking pussy to your ass. Your mind is already drawn into me completely, as you submerge your limp body weakening, wanting, mind, soul, heart, spirit as you completely submit yourself to me. As you surrender yourself unto me one hundred percent as I take control over everything you are sexually with a desire with the flame of ecstasy that will never go out. You are in a very deep erotic sexual trance that takes you to paradise. You so willing give and surrender your sexual desires to me and become a very obedient; submissive woman with no hesitation as our spirits merges together. Now come to your Master with no restraint and give unto him what he desires from you my submissive play thing.

LAST DRINK BEFORE I DIE:

I live to play, I live to have fun I'll drink in my whiskey.

Baby please why don't you stay help me drink away.

I'm running because I've got the blues. Why don't you help me get the clues? I'm running because I’ve got the blues while drinking my whiskey away.

I was made to love with a good woman at my side. But yet we got so far to go before the whistle blows.

So, we better make our way at the end of the day. We can say what a ride this was a time to remember.

I keep on keeping on with these eyes. Not knowing how much time I have before I die.

So, baby please be in my loving arms tonight as we break free.

Chapter 4

SEARCHING TO LIVE:

I don't know what I'm searching for.

Or who I'm looking for?

Do I even know who I am?

Walking down the road living day to day.

Wondering if my path is paved all's I can remember is my past as the hurt comes back.

Am I living from day to day?

I pray that God takes me away!

Each day I'm dying inside even though I try to live.

There is nothing more to give, what more do I have to prove? what more is to be said?

Part of me is dead, the other part is I am alive, I'm in between both worlds lost in a parallel spinning around on a carousel.

Want to go off like a cannon. Emotion all over the place while everyone points out my mistakes, I pray for someone to come but no one is this there I'm in a Black hole, I'm in black hole.

BROKEN TO BE MISFITTED:

I am broken never been wanted by anyone.

Left abandoned into desolate isolation. Been tossed around by everyone I have ever met. Never understood and always been looked down being a misfitted creature out of a lab. Unloved, unwanted, thrown away like a piece of trash always an outcast; past coming back to haunt me I will never be free.

My tears keep me locked away,

It's the anger that has fed me and keeps me alive.

Walls are up to never be broken down always despised.

My Life is like living on the seas in a storm first its calm then chaos unfolds disorder abrupt in my life not knowing which direction to go but being tossed by the wind. Oh where will I land?

NOTHING TO HAVE:

I came from nothing,

No one ever gave me anything.

Barley had any food in the house.

I barely can remember my childhood.

Being bullied every day of my life inside of school and outside from the home.

But it was inside the home where it was the worst.

Now I'm a grown man standing on my own two feet, with my head held up high wearing a badge of pride. Knowing I made it, even with all of the self-doubt.

Oh Lord please help me keep holding on.

BOTTOM SHELF LOVE:

You and I make magic when we're together.

Don't want nobody to bother us.

Let's take the night away as I gaze up at the stars, I see your eyes in the sky,

As I go about looking for pleasure I look to you and realize you ain't top shelf quality you bottom shelf flavor, good enough to get my rocks off as I get drunk.

(verse 1)

In this dive bar haze, I search for pleasure's,

Embrace,

But you, my dear, ain’t top shelf grace.

You’re that bottom shelf flavour, but that's,

Alright,

Cause you're just enough to keep me

Warm at night.

(Chorus)

You're my bottom shelf love, in this neon,
Light,
A cheap thrill, but it feels so right.
As I drown in this whisky, feeling so high,
You're my bottom shelf love, "'neath the Tennessee sky".

(Verse 2)

You might not be the smoothest, or the
Finest poor,
But your fire burns within, and I want more
With every sip, I lose myself in you,
In this tangled mess of love, we both pursue.

(Chorus)

You're my bottom shelf love, in this neon
Light
A cheap thrill, but it feels so right
As I drown in this whisky, feeling so high,
You're my bottom shelf love, "'neath the Tennessee sky".

(Bridge)

In the moonlights glow, we dance this

Night away,

Two souls entwined, come what may

Bottom shelf or top, it doesn’t really matter,

As long as we're together, it’s all that fated to scatter

(Chorus)

You’re my bottom shelf love, in this neon

Light

A cheap thrill, but it feels so right

As I drown in this whisky, feeling so high,

You’re my bottom shelf love, "‘neath the Tennessee sky"

NO BELIEVE:

Never had a chance.

Never had a beginning.

Always been at the grind.

It never hurts to be kind.

I thank God every day for whom I am and not what my past taught me to be.

My life is living by the pain inside,

Want to yell and scream why can't my life be changed. I tried religion what can change in my life?

what is the meaning of my life in this world?

I have raised above of what others, have told me what I couldn't be. Always down on myself always hard on myself giving into self-doubt but the strength that's is in me will never let me give up.

I'm not going to look at what I have lost, I am going to look at what I have gained.

Even in the times of trouble blessings have been in my life.

EMOTION OF A PERSON:

We all have a spirit we all have a soul

We all live and breathe.

With hearts pumping and blood flowing.

We love, We hate,

We are vulnerable, We also come together.

We try not to put over on anyone but at times we feel jealous of others.

The strength that is in us tells us to push on to keep moving forward it's the drive of not giving up no matter how hard it gets no matter how rich or poor we are. It's the humanity that gives us life so never give up, keep putting one foot in front of the other, continue to evolve let's get problems solved. Let’s continue to live not only for ourselves but for others as well. Kindness and love are what everyone could use.

That's a beautiful sentiment. Kindness and love can truly make a difference in our lives and in the lives of others.

It’s important to remember that we are all connected and that by showing compassion and understanding, we can create a more harmonious world. Let's continue to support each other, uplift one another, and work together to overcome challenges and make a positive impact.

PROFOUND OF TEMPTATION CAN'T HOLD BACK:

My world is fire wake up and smoke weed.

I get to go to work as I plant seeds.

Driving in a car with no ac getting blazed by the sun as I'm getting cooked.

I get hooked when I see a phat ass goes by just want to jump and go to town see how long she can go pound for pound.

When the deed is done, we get some drink pour it down we have fun then we go our separate ways go on about our day.

(Verse 1)

In a world ablaze, wake up, let the smoke weave,

Planting seeds, heading to work, life's reprieve.

No AC in the car, sun's a fiery embrace,

Getting cooked, getting blazed, in this hectic race.

(Chorus)

Phat ass strollin' by, temptation profound,
Jump and go to town, pound for pound.
Deeds are done, pour a drink, let it flow,
Fun's begun, then we part, let life's river go.

(Verse 2)

Highways and byways, a journey untold,
In the heat of the moment, our stories unfold.
Chasing moments, living in the present,
Lost in the rhythm, life's sweet descent.

(Bridge)

Smoke and mirrors, a dance in the haze,
Lost in the maze of life's fleeting phase.
Phat ass memories linger and play,
As we part ways, continue our own way.

(Chorus)

Phat ass strollin' by, temptation profound,
Jump and go to town, pound for pound.
Deeds are done, pour a drink, let it flow,
Fun's begun, then we part, let life's river go.

(Outro)

Sunsets and highways, our paths diverge,
A fleeting encounter, a tale on the verge.
In the echo of moments, we find our way,
As the rhythm of life continues to sway.

TRAVLED DOWN THE ROAD:

I have travelled down the road,

And nothing seems to keep me company.

The only thing that is at my side is my shadow.

Wake up lonely in the night and ensuring the day.

All's, I wanted to be is picked up but nobody sees me.

I wanted to be in the light but pushed into the darkness learning from my demons.

Been forgotten about, unseen, unheard, of pushed back falling into the cracks. Stepped over swept underneath the rug, redactable, unchangeable, unseen, unchangeable doesn't matter what I've done, I've always been thrown across into the garbage. I'm a nobody where no one hears my words; all of my words fall onto deaf ears always been told I was a piece of shit not going anywhere. But I'm right here I'm still standing you tried to hold me down onto your level but I rose above you I'm better than you. I feel I'm hopeless nobody ever needed me. I'm never heard always being cut down no one there to save me.

Thought Who is here to help me not too cross the line? I'm in between mine own mind, which is heaven or hell? Thoughts are tormenting me living back as child in my adult mind. The neglect and abuse stay with me until the day I die.

PASSIONS OF A MERE THOUGHT:

You are my mere thought when I wake first thing in the morning, you are with me all day and when I go to sleep. I imagine your skin caressing my skin as your silk hands run on my body and as your sweet tender lips softly kiss my lips below my waist. My hands gently keep you comfort as my warmth protects you as my arms embraces you and make you feel safe as you and your body melts right into me with passion stronger than you have ever felt. You just completely surrender yourself without hesitation and rest in my bosom.

In the dawn's embrace, you're my waking thought,
A presence lingering, all day you're sought.
Silk hands caress in the evening's soft glow,
Sweet lips below my waist, a tender flow.
In the warmth of my arms, comfort you find,
Passion stronger than ever, heart and mind.
Surrendering completely, hesitation cast,
Resting in my bosom, a love unsurpassed.

STORY OF REGRETS:

There is no story to tell cause my life has been so cold,
it’s hard to speak when your lips are frozen shut.
This is my song story as it continues to be maddening
sometimes. I wish I would have disappeared to be
amongst the stars.
So tired so many regrets I wish I could be far away but
I’m trapped in another reality. It feels like gravity is
pulling me downward into a sandpit.
So much pain with life's stains do not know what to do in
my head all day workin myself into the ground.
Mother I have no mother,
A Father is nowhere to be found.
Can’t cope with life, constant pressure pushing down on
me can’t be free,
No one taught me to see.

BEAUTY OF SPIRITS MERGING TOGETHER:

Your beauty has no bounds as it reaches from the west to the east. From the north to the south. It is in awe struck that has me paralyzed with no words to say. Our energy matches one another as our Spirits have been intertwined together since the beginning of creation. We have not crossed paths because this is the time that is meant to be for us. As we cannot survive without water as I cannot survive without you, I can't separate what is and what will be but this I know that you are to be part of me to make a whole you are my half and this I do know. Our power and energy shall be as one to an unfold with a bond that has been stronger than we both have ever felt. This is beyond Our flesh but of our spirits emerging together with an unreliquinshly of hope stronger than we have ever felt. You are my past my present and my future. Our flesh shall merge together and become one. We are enslaved into one another. Journeys are walked by ourselves with goals to accomplish but adventures are meant to be shared to burden with one another to hold each other up with a path that has obstacles in the way but at times it is to be cleared to walk straight away.

NO BODY AROUND:

I have nobody to talk too.

No body to listen to speak my mind.

For what is to be said just so I can get a peace of mind.

Everybody always fakes to be kind so they can throw their troubles onto you.

Weak is what they think.

But they forget to realize that I have become a nightmare to scare you even in the air down and out. I have got nothing to lose as now I become your living nightmare.

Do it all again to me cause I'll haunt you in your dreams.

UNKNOWN ROAD AHEAD:

As we walk the unknown road ahead as I am scared, I just sing your name and it gives me strength. But I don't know where we are headed but we got each other no matter the cost but I know now we walk this journey together with the unknown road ahead.

To the power of words,

Word is my bond so strong that it cannot be wronged my words seals my soul to yours.

Let my voice echo in your heart

Let my words pierce your soul to. draw closer to me let me LOVE YOU as you need.

Let my presence be your strength let my touch paralyze you into my arms as our Love.

Give into me as I have Given into you for no longer is the fight of a struggle but submerging into the strength of the Love that is in me that is in you, I can no Longer bear but only to give into.

Chapter 5

IMMERSE OF ILLUSION:

Self-destruction with the immerse of illusion is the hate that is inside, it comes out to play as my life is being destroyed.

Lived my life in Denial being in box of delusion.

I'm the one who's self-destruction, learning how to reconstruct myself only to lose my mind why am I a freak? why am I the way I am? I want to change but I can't.

Just want to jump off the edge to end it all.

I have to fight to lose it all.

Just want to take off and take flight,

No one is coming for you.

Your alone in your own darkness.

I want to hide away hide away.

The weight is crushing me.

HEAD BOMB OF RADIO REMIX:

I've got a head bomb full of radio
I'm reusable recyclable.

Let me use your love as we are strangers in my bed, I want more of ya.
I want to lay you down, play mind control until your body starts to explode.
Let the lights be off as we start to unfold.

Let me touch you,
Want to control you,
Contribute your body to me there is no scolding, only free folding in the land of ecstasy.
I Like the rising of your vibrations.

OUTCAST OF A LONER:

I'm a loner no matter where I have been.

I'm an outcast no matter whom I'm with.

Always seems that I'm alone as I roam.

What's the cause of loneliness? That everyone abandoned me. Only so much hurt being ripped out of me.

Playing my own character in my own show of being obscured.

I don't have a good bloodline there is something away I don't know what. I'm missing been gone for so long I am astray in the streets. It doesn't matter how much I have prayed. I have nothing to say everything is in the wind. The wind wipes the tears away.

My being at war with in myself tearing conflict of my soul, spirit torn apart, don't know what to do any more. Just make me into a war machine, war is ugly, war is pain, war is death nobody wants me this black Sunday in a mass of black witches' at the black masses. I try to hang on but only to be revered by other people having only to hold onto hate. The only shield I can wield is the one full of rage with vengeance with hate. I have been crucified for who I am. I can really never trust any one.

Song: EROTIC STIMULATION OF DRSIRE:

Allow the mind to go into a state of erotic stimulating arousal. As your sexual desire becomes more stronger with every thought, with every movement of a touch as my voice paralyzes you. As you are helpless only able to move just a bit only able to follow commands from hearing my voice. Your body is flooded with your juices just by my presence as I begin to touch you in ways that you never been touched before. It's different it means something more than you realize. The sensation of sexual erotic play you submerge into a subconscious that you presently come into my will my sexual loving woman. The uncontrollable of the sexual demons coming out is unbearable of not getting enough as we are away from one another it’s that drive that keeps bringing you back into my world.

Song: DIRTY EROTIC PLEASURE;

Making a sexual organic erotic ecstasy pleasure of enjoying every inch of your holes every touch of your body and mind. Mind play is weakening you into my bosom as you are being toyed with your ass. Your pussy seeks to be dominated into pleasure as you as you look at me your memorized desperate puppy eyes as to look to her Master. Come and enjoy the pleasure of the company that I present.

Let your world unfold into the grasp of my bosom Let your eroticism come to play as you are taken into whole nether world that you have never been too.

Song: PLEASURABLE EYE CANDY:

The site of whom I am; in your eyes The sound of my voice with the base in the tone that gets your mind going as the tingling trickles down to your pussy as you start to get wet uncontrollable, follow the smell of my body that sets your sexual ecstasy desire off as your body tingles with every movement. All your muscle start to tighten up as your pussy is wet down to your ass. As you think of me sexually Your sexual desire gets stronger and stronger as I am on your mind with every step. In every move you make, you have no choice but to surrender it unto me.

STORMY STEPS OF LIFE:

I have stormed my steps in front of one another with it not being of any kind of breeze. Life has been lived, is not with any kind of ease. A hard lived life has always been with some kind of strife and consequence.

There have been heart aches with hardships with no everlasting trips.

Life is full of time sequences that is filled with holes that are never to be filled but to remain a dark abyss.

No one around No one to be found I'm alone with no assets.

Finally, I lay my head down and pray I can finally be at peace be no more as I am to be a-miss.

STRONGER OF BEING ALONE:

As I walk alone, I really never knew how strong a person could be until defeat has beaten me to the point of my blast breath.

It is the sole mere thought of isolation, around me even though I am completely free to move about. Certain situations have told me the complete opposite of what I have been told all of my life. Life its self has told me that I can stand alone in any situation and still thrive because I know how to stand alone when there is nobody else to draw strength from. God has truly blessed me in life and through every situation that I have been through. I have stood tall I have stood low had many victories and many defeats. But all in all, I know I can stand by myself with God by my side not because of my faith that gives me strength but just knowing that I can keep pushing and not giving up.

DANCE OF LIFE:

Deep into the night there's terror walking along minding my own business and outcomes the horror,

I have danced the dance of life in all the selfish fun of the flesh. I have twirled around the flaming fire of sin and destruction. The pleasantries of this life have torn my family apart because of selfish desires that I have entertained in my life of the king of being solo when I am truly am not. The lies I have endured of ruining one's life. I have walked away from God pleasing myself when it has destroyed me, not only me but my family. I am coming back to God because I can no longer do it anymore. I truly do love my family and now I'm afraid of what is to be. But no matter what I do believe in God still stands my faith still stands.

Mourning in my own grief for that I myself has caused as I live with it as well as the enduring affliction.

NOTHING MORE THAN A MEMORY:

I am nothing more than a distant memory in the breath of the winds that is blowing in the air from one distance to another. There is nothing more in my heart than vanity and displacement on the ground that I stand on.

My mere presence single handily sparks of resentment and bitterness of the urgency that surrounds me.

There are no safe guards that behold me but definite utter ruins that seem to sink in deeper and deeper with not one word to speak out for I fear it only falls on deaf ears.

The only thing that is reliable is silence in your own fortitude within the parameters of one self-inside your soul along with your own thoughts. It is not the day nor the night that brings one into self-loathing but it is the acts of people who are against you in the manner of your own self and of your presence. The importance of one self is no more than a mere of a facade; of an illusion that the world has manipulated upon one's mind.

PLOTTING TO CONSPIRE ON A POOR BOY:

Ever since I was a youngster always been poor, my eyes have seen violence with nowhere to run nowhere to turn. Always feeling hunger in my stomach always felt humiliated, always embarrassed, each time I look around people gossiping plotting to conspire.

Instead of being the influence with desire there is nothing I require. Except your friendship, but even that has a price even at my expense of my character and of my being. It feels like a mission every week so now, I turn to with what I have seen. Now the violence has to come in and play, play into me so I don't feel weak anymore. I'm choosing my side to protect my soul cause you know the devil is out for blood looking for control. Nobody to trust everyone is corrupt. Now is the time to start blowing up know how deeply God sees into your heart I know he's never too far apart.

DARKNESS IS WHAT I KNOW:

Black is dark, dark is cold,

I reach out to the empty vastness

Feel nothing there only to fold.

An empty shell is what I am, what have I become since I have failed?

Lonely is my soul with nothing to hold.

The darkness is my world not knowing if I'm in between heaven or hell.

Am I being in an illusion of my own demise?

Cold is what I breath, cold is what I am the struggle of living or dying.

Black is cold, black is dark, cold is what I am.

DEATH HAS SOUGHT ME:

Long into this life as death has sought me out; as I have been resistant unto obliging.

The unforgiving thought of losing myself and resting into his bosom. The blossoming of a once a young man's soul has grown weary, weak, demoralized, and grim. As one continues to put one foot in front of the other not knowing when the last footstep will be, his last along with the whisper of his breath that carries his voice. Whispers begins to fade into silence and all that is left are thoughts in his head that no one will ever hear. Longing for something more that will never be reached it is the unsettling thought of not being able to break the silent sounds of the dark nor the still quietness.

WONDERING SOULESS:

I thought I have been soulless because of aimlessly wondering about not knowing where to go. Nothing to hold onto and nothing to gloat; foundation weekend at its core my mind and body so tired that I'm sore not even to move a muscle. Thinking I have been forgotten about, always being put on the back burner. Why do I always must suffer? Why do I get thrown underneath to the winds of destruction?

With every step just take everything in as I continue. All of whom I am being ostracized from society.

Never really belonged to anyone or anything. The days seem to get greyer and darker along with storm clouds getting heavier and bigger. As the days come and go, I ask myself are these the last days for me? Every time I turn my head, I'm hated for who I am.

PRESSURE OF A LONG HARD ROAD:

The road has been long and hard never easy to endure as my feet have wondered for so long that they are bleeding. Trying to stop the blood from flowing no matter how hard the pressure is, the bleeding just won't stop.

Then all of the sudden my heart drops I gasp for air but nothing can be caught, nothing can be done, no matter how hard I have fought. The pain is real the emptiness is eating me alive, loneliness is the only thing I have to keep me company with my shadow.

I wish I could roll up my problems and wish them away I write them down on a piece of paper and pray. As I pray my life away I've gone too far astray living life from day to day not knowing what's going to happen so here is my body that lies down to a still rest.

Chapter 6

SMOKE AND MIRRORS WHILE I RUN:

I walk in pain I run while hurting my dreams.

My dreams are collapsed where I was fortified, as I lie awake grasp the reality around me; I'm mortified at life as it has a strange hold on me, unsolidified carrying rage with in my soul. I was taught to care about the world that surrounds me and the people with whom it brings. Yet the people near me have always turned on me. Not one soul to trust with in the distance of what I can see. Everything is smoke and mirrors, now reach as far as you can. Each time I take a step to reach out I'm alone, I fall on my face cause I've been betrayed with backs turned away from me now all's I have, is fear from all of those whom are around me, whom have betrayed me; now I don't care.

Won't show mercy no matter how bad you bleed.

In my head I hear I am not dead you are alive keep fighting to survive, keep pushing, no regrets never give up. In my head I hear I am not dead, you are alive keep fighting to survive, keep stomping, keep pushing never to give up. Keep your head up walk step by step. The struggle of life is with our own decisions. I'm a reviving person from my birth I should have been dead. No one even wanted to count the number of hairs that was on my head, no one cared who I was or when I was born and no one cares who I am now. As a human, as a man, I am replaceable. It does not matter how hard you work or how much you give, at the end of the day what does it really matter anyway? What does it truly mean? All you have in this world is yourself, your word. You are just another body that is added to the count of endlessness.

CRAZY LIFE but FUN:

Life is fun life is crazy,
I see through you like jelly,
Bring it down, bring it low,
How high can you rise?
Do you taste like apple butter jam?
Or do you taste like strawberries?
Reach back slap it back!
Let's pop the mattress,
Shootin up in the club,
Break ya back for me!
Come here let me talk to ya.
Hear what's whispered in your ear.
Life is fun Life is crazy,
Let me get ya twisted,
Get ya all nice and hazy ain't no need to get lazy.
Come and get yourself exploded, I'll work,
You so hard you will be imploded.
Show me Let's give ya lick of your

Strawberries. Let me have a taste what I have tasted.
Let's head back home as we keep the flow,
Hit the gas pedal, to see how well you can take all this metal. Lets just go, like to see if you taste like candy or sweet apple butter jam.
You lookin at the best there ain't no need to be looking for the rest you will be ripped up by nights end you just won't be able to get enough.

SONG: MATCHING HURTS

Matching ain't matchin tried to get over but it didn't work out.

The math ain't mathin I'm just cold at heart.

The drugs ain't drugin and now I feel the pain.

I'm flying high off of adrenaline, nothing will be the same again.

Coming down into depression Life is holding me in suppression.

Life is just an illusion my head hurts with all of this confusion.

Want to go off into paradise.

In all my ways I've just rolled the dice

I don't know why, why, why.

I can't get out of my own way,

As I fall back into the same ol pattern

Feel like nothing does not matter,

I don't know why, why, oh, oh, ho, why, oh why.

A GRAND SCHEME OF LIFE:

I work hard for my family even though they barely see me.

Never had anyone to hold me.

Never had anyone in my corner,

Never did I have a father to tell me son it's OK to struggle.

Always finding myself in a muddy puddle. Thing doesn't seem to change in this game of life. But I pray one day my kids will see how hard I worked for them and to see that I never gave up no matter how hard things got:

(Verse 1)

I work hard for my family, they don't see me much,

In this life's storm, I've been feeling out of touch,

No one to hold me, no one in my corner,

No father's voice to say, "Son, it's okay to falter."

(Pre-Chorus)

But I keep pushing forward, through the darkest night,

In this endless struggle, I'll keep up the fight.

(Chorus)

I'm in this muddy puddle, it's a never-ending game,
But I pray my kids will see my love, my burning flame,
I won't give up, no matter how tough it gets,
For them, I'll break these chains, I'll never have regrets.

(Verse 2)

I've faced countless trials, in this life's grand scheme,
But through the pain and tears, I'll keep on chasing dreams,
Though the road is rocky, and the journey's long,
I'll stand tall for my family; I'll prove them wrong.

(Pre-Chorus)

I keep pushing forward, through the darkest night,
In this endless struggle, I'll keep up the fight.

(Chorus)

I'm in this muddy puddle, it's a never-ending game,
But I pray my kids will see my love, my burning flame,

I won't give up, no matter how tough it gets,
For them, I'll break these chains, I'll never have regrets.

(Bridge)
Through the storms and thunder, I'll be their guiding light,
I'll keep the flame burning, in the darkest of nights,
They'll know I never quit, no matter how things got,
For my family's love, I'll give it all I've got.

(Chorus)
I'm in this muddy puddle, it's a never-ending game,
But I pray my kids will see my love, my burning flame,
I won't give up, no matter how tough it gets,
For them, I'll break these chains, I'll never have regrets.

(Outro)
Through the struggles of life, I'll always find a way,
For my family's sake, I'll keep the darkness at bay,

I'll keep pushing forward, in the face of strife,

For my kids, I'll be their hero, I'll be their guiding light.

This a saying before the song. A quote:

COUNT ON YOURSELF:

Things work out til they don’t.

Your useful only for the needs at that time. You come in dime a dozen. In for a moment for those around you only for them to betray.

(Verse 1)

Things work out 'til they don't,
Useful for the needs, in time you won't,
Dime a dozen, here for a moment,
Betrayed by those you thought were potent.

(Chorus)

Count on yourself and trust in God,
He'll reveal what you're made of,
Falling not knowing where you'll land,
Strength and courage lift you, take a stand.

(Verse 2)

One foot in front, one step at a time,
Legacy whispers, "Don't give up," in rhyme,
Hold on tight, keep the stronghold,
In the journey of life, let your story unfold.

(Bridge)

Through twists and turns, you'll find your way,
Learn from each stumble, seize the day,
Challenges faced, make you strong,
In the melody of life, sing your song.

(Chorus)

Count on yourself and trust in God,
He'll reveal what you're made of,
Falling not knowing where you'll land,
Strength and courage lift you, take a stand.

(Outro)

So, don't give up, let your legacy shine,

With each sunrise, a new chapter you'll find,

In the rhythm of hope, your heart beats strong,

This song of resilience, forever your song.

LETTER TO GOD:

This is how letters used to start let me give you an example so let's begin this lesson:

Without any tension here I am going on a mission for once without any condition here we go here we go.

Dear God so many things that I need to ask: how can parents of children be so abusive to the point where they destroy their hopes dreams only to kill them?

Help me to know what's wrong.

I can't get away from my past,

I know good days don't last.

Tried to pray I tried to run away.

But at the end of the day, I'm tired and frayed.

Why did you have to let the frame work be so abusive that my brother had to take his own life why?

How come people have to hate? Why is it that religion is always a debate? I am now a grown man and taught to pro create is that fate?

Straight out of the gate everything is turned upside down. We all are on a merry go round with no way out. I have nothing left to do except to stand up and shout to let everything I'm feeling out.

Dear God: Why is there always hate? Temptation all around me it is nothing but bate. Why does this world have to destroy everything you created? Let's just not sit there and congregate let's us migrate.

The Late hour of the day:

The hour is late the day is dimming

Grey and dark appear.

As I no longer live in fear.

Combat weapons and guns at the ready,

In my hands

I call on my brothers in arms ready and armed,

As we take our stand,

To Plunder no surrender is in our blood.

I'm tired of running and being afraid!

I'm making this into my destiny.

To go ashore on the winds of my ancestors to hear my heed. Let my echoes be heard through the winds of life's destiny oh ho oh

Let my footprints be seen.

As the winds carry me,

I'm being called to Eternity;

Being called to eternity;

As the winds carry me I'M BEING CALLED TO ENTERNITY.

Manipulation of Corruptintion of the Soul:

Once a Broken soul has been torn apart,

It's nearly impossible to heal.

You grow cold as you learn not to feel.

Some people have asked why did you turn heel? I answered "Cause no one cared"!

No one dared to hold me,

I learned on my own as I have gone.

People are corrupt.

Manipulation is at the root of others Intentions.

No one is there for you.

So, you've got to hold true to yourself.

My soul has been torn apart again,

Don't have any friends, so now I have turned heel to get you back for all the harm you caused. Left me with no choice but to fail to die.

I have tried to pry myself from the terror that has haunted me, but I can't break away freely, never truly free from my own hell.

When do the bells ring again?
Where am I going to end up with a shattered life?
Let my story tell others not to be like me.
Cause I’m a lost cause my sorrow ate me up, into the ground I go.

Trapped in my own demise:

Endless days, sleepless nights
At the end of it all what really matters?
When my might is gone,
Trapped in my own mind full of mazes of which I cannot escape.
Judging of what has become before
This time, this day, this hour.
There is no more, that is not new it's all the same.
As it comes in different forms;
There is no Quorum here.
The Quarl is of my own demise,
There is no rise, There is no fall
But we are born to die, Struggle grips a hold of me I have yet to be free from the muddy struggle.
The days are grey, the light around me is grim.
Are my days getting shorter? Very little time.

As my mind fades sadden is the tears, of a broken man as he becomes of the dust. As the wind sweeps away the ashes of bones for once the man is at peace.

God's light and Devils Dark:

I've played with the devil dance in around the fire.

I've walked with God's Angels and spoken with them on a day that is higher than any other day.

My life has been shovelled around as I'm nowhere to be found.

Under the moon light is where I keep my secrets.

In the day light is where I pray as my feet are on the ground.

After all I have done is there any salvation for me? Or am I Condemned to go underneath?

One day the sun will set what will happen then?

Working hard:

Light rider, pain pill seeker while listing to seether,
aggressive violator, nurse user,
Doing what I can to get the job done
Keep getting interrupted only wishing I had a gun.
Full of surprises thinking to myself why is this no fun oh
why can't I win the lottery only to be done.
Mental capacity is on the fringe of agony while my nerves
are anxiously waiting for me to be stabbed in the back
only to irrupt angrily but have to put on a smile to be fake
admirably knowing that there is no cavalry.
Hey let me go on a narcotics binge from the pills only to
wash it down with a bottle of whisky only to get the chills.

Seasons of change:

I have not been forgiven for the things I've done.
Been hated on just for who I have been.
Never been forgiven for my mistakes,
Stuck here for life don't know where to go from here.
I've put all of my effort into it
But nothing comes out.
Spent my whole life being broken.
Working to make things better
But life has a way of keeping you down.
Keeping your mood in the same space
I try to make the pain go away.
Popping pills, drinking getting drunk, getting high, getting drunk go off to a different universe wondering what a whole new place would be like living a whole new life dreaming about the changes.
I feel the season is coming,
No one calls, no one says hi,
I'm not on ice my feet are held to the fire.

It's hard to know how to live when you really haven't known life.
I wish I was more than what I am!
In shadows of mistakes, forgiveness yet eludes,
Hated for being, misunderstood and accused.
Life's path unclears, a prisoner of my past,
Struggling in silence, uncertain and cast.

Effort expended, yields naught in return,
A lifetime of brokenness, a ceaseless concern.
Facing adversity, to make things right,
Yet life's heavy hand keeps me in the night.

Pills and drinks, a fleeting escape,
Chasing a high, a different landscape.
Dreaming of a realm where change takes flight,
Seeking solace in the arms of the night.

Seasons change, but solitude persists,
No calls, no greetings, an emptiness persists.
Feet held to the fire, a relentless pyre,
In the midst of life's unforgiving mire.

Yearning for more, a desire to transcend,
To be more than this, to break and mend.
Yet, in the unknown, a hopeful spark,
A chance for a rebirth, a journey to embark.

Rockin Rythem, Good Lovin:

Good lovin tonight,
The Rockin don't stop.
And the parting doesn't quit

(Verse 1)
In the moonlight's glow, feeling just right,
Good lovin' tonight, let's dance through the night.
The rhythm's alive, the Rockin' won't cease,
Our hearts beating in sync, a melody of peace.

(Chorus)
Good lovin' tonight, the Rockin' won't stop,
Partying hard, till the morning's first drop.
No time to quit, let the music play on,
In this moment, our worries are gone.

(Verse 2)
Underneath the stars, where dreams take flight,
The groove is electric, igniting the night.

A symphony of laughter, as we reminisce,
In the dance of joy, our worries we dismiss.

(Chorus)
Good lovin' tonight, the Rockin' won't stop,
Partying hard, till the morning's first drop.
No time to quit, let the music play on,
In this moment, our worries are gone.

(Bridge)
Guitar strings strumming, a beat so divine,
In the rhythm of love, our souls intertwine.
The party's alive, in the embrace of the sound,
Lost in the music, we're forever bound.

(Verse 3)
The night is our canvas, let's paint it bright,
With laughter and joy, till the morning light.
The dance floor's calling, a magnetic force,
In the world of music, we find our source.

(Chorus)

Good lovin' tonight, the Rockin' won't stop,
Partying hard, till the morning's first drop.
No time to quit, let the music play on,
In this moment, our worries are gone.

(Outro)

As the night bids farewell, and the music subsides,
Memories linger, in the rhythm that guides.
Good lovin' tonight, etched in our hearts,
A melody of joy, where the soul imparts.

REALM OF LIFE:

What am I cut out for?

I'm a working man barely providing for my family I fight like hell just to keep my head above the water.

I'm still in the realm of life, I search my purpose's lore,

A working soul, striving to provide for family I adore.

Battling fiercely, against currents I endeavour,

Just to keep my head above the water, forever.

Busy like a honeybee:

I don't want to work no more,

I want to go home,

Tired of the workday.

Get a drink or too in;

Then kiss my honey and get busy like a honeybee.

I like the way you lick those lips

Love to feel the way you shake them hips girl.

I Love it when we make those trips together.

When I'm alone don't have anyone to hold.

I'm cryin I'm crying yes baby I'm cryin for you.

(Verse 1)

I'm done with the grind, can't take it no more,

Yearning for home, that's where I wanna go.

Tired of the workday, it's dragging me down,

A couple of drinks in, let the worries drown.

(Pre-Chorus)
Kiss my honey, get busy like a honeybee,
Lost in the moment, just you and me.

(Chorus)
I like the way you lick those lips,
Feel the rhythm as you shake those hips.
Together on trips, memories unfold,
When I'm alone, no one to hold.

(Verse 2)
Crying in silence, baby, it's true,
I'm yearning, I'm longing, all for you.
No one compares to the love we share,
In your arms, I find comfort rare.

(Pre-Chorus)
Kiss my honey, get busy like a honeybee,
Lost in the moment, just you and me.

(Chorus)
I like the way you lick those lips,
Feel the rhythm as you shake those hips.
Together on trips, memories unfold,
When I'm alone, no one to hold.

(Bridge)
Through ups and downs, we'll navigate,
Our love's a journey, don't underestimate.
Hold me close, wipe away the tears,
In your embrace, overcome the fears.

(Chorus)
I like the way you lick those lips,
Feel the rhythm as you shake those hips.
Together on trips, memories unfold,
When I'm alone, no one to hold.

(Outro)

So, let’s keep dancing, through laughter and tears,

In this symphony of love, conquering our fears.

No more crying, just joy anew,

Forever bound, me and you.

AMERICA ON A WAR PATH:

America is on a war path it has always been a race war, it has never been, any equal to black people or people of different colour of origin. America could be what it could be, a home for many that could be so much greater if the tyranny of the heart ceases to hate. Oh how the mighty crushes the weak and drives the poor soles of every race and of every origin out of its place out of the house. They cause the black culture and other culture of different origins to feel less than when its the complete opposite if history is told right. Don't you hear the pain that cries out in the agony of a culture of many people who have been travailing since 1690. How diversity of other cultures that people have such scars how the immigrants been in such disarray and Strip by governments; family's are being destroyed by the mere stench of ignorance. Let what the land of liberty shout out our freedom and equality as the air we breathe let this land be of no Faults but of patriotic love for those who seek it. Let equality ring as Liberty sings for those who need to breathe it for life and for strength young men and young women. Who are full of strength and hope and faith keep fighting. Never back down don't let the wealth of those who grab the gold who seek to gain profit and power to grab the land to grab and take to have for one selfish greed, to suppress those under them. You don't have the gold or riches let this bloody endless chain cease. That has been single a moto for over 400 years. Let the farmer who has to till the land that he works for you, but the rich keeps beating him down and he gets back up to work. The black culture has been here forced too serve even though they dare to dream, and to make something of him or herself. Despite the American dream, it is still made to be torn away only to add more scars to the old ones the mighty negro the immigrant and the poor and all stand in unison, together to raise their voice in a one accord. In harmony and in one heart beat we will not be defeated we will be strong, we will keep marching. The more you take the stronger we become the more you beat us down the more stronger the people become. One voice and one fight as we all will be heard our voices. Our Sons and Daughters blood will be heard and stretched across the skies freedom and equality will ring we will be brave we will be strong and we will be brave; Who said we will be free?

Who made America?

Whose faith gave songs to America?

Whose history gave America?

Let us never forget the dream of America. Let it burn a fire in people's soul's to live for. Let us live for Freedom and Equality, but not let us never forget for those who have died for the struggle and the blood that has been spilled that was so unnecessary.

Chapter 7

BROKEN BRIDGES:

I'm having so much fun can't you see?

I am doing things I should not do,

I say things I should not say.

I drink things I should not drink.

Living a life full of regrets.

(Verse 1)

I'm having so much fun, can't you see?

But I'm losing myself, it's not just me.

Doing things I shouldn't do, oh so wrong,

I'm singing this song, but it's been too long.

(Chorus)

I say things I should not say,

I drink things I should not drink,

Living a life full of regrets,

It's time to change, to redirect.

(Verse 2)

I've danced in the darkness, lost my way,
But now I see the light, it's a brand-new day.

Gotta breaks these chains, find a better view,
I'm leaving behind the old, embracing what's true.

(Chorus)

I say things I should not say,
I drink things I should not drink,
Living a life full of regrets,
It's time to change, to redirect.

(Bridge)

I'll mend these broken bridges,
I'll climb these walls so high.
No more living in the shadows,
I'll spread my wings; I'll fly.

(Chorus)

I say things I should not say,
I drink things I should not drink,
Living a life full of regrets,
It's time to change, to redirect.

(Outro)

I'm breaking free from my mistakes,
A better life is what I'll make.
No more living with regret,
I'll rise above, I won't forget.

LIFE'S TOO SHORT:

Simplified is what I like to live by.
No tellin what will come or what will go.
What today will bring? Or what tomorrow will sing?
What is there to think besides sitting down to nice hard drink?
What am I getting into my life?
How am I feeling tonight with the moonlight beaming down on me?

Let's have a drink together with friends.
Raise a glass let our worries take flight,

With friends around were on the brink of a night we won't forget that's for sure let's write a story with thousands of words as we speak life.

What am I getting into my world of wonder and strife?
I'm dancing to the rythem that my heart brings.

What today will bring? What tomorrow will sing? Let's dance to the rhythm that our hearts bring, Raise a glass and let our worries take flight under the moonlight, worries take flight under the moonlight, we’ll be alright).

LOST IN ENDLESS NIGHT

What the hell am I?
Where the hell can I go?
Been holding my breath,
Just surviving of my own survival,
Nearly missing death.
I have put my feet on the ground today.
But I don't know about tomorrow
I'm tired of hurting tired of burning,
Whom am I lost in this endless night?
Where can I find myself in this fight? holding my breath cleaning to my own survival.
Dancing on the edge escaping fates cruel revival.
Today I stand firm on the ground but tomorrow paths of uncertainty are bound.
I'm weary about this pain with nothing else to gain.
The fire is in me to seek solace and peace to lift my spirits higher.

WEB OF KNOTS:

What I got is tangled up mess that's knotted up in mesh.

Oh I can't believe that in this threshold of webs that has gotten me all tied up.

Days like today are blessings.

In the tangled mesh, a mess unfurls,

Knots of life in a web that swirls.

Threshold of webs, a dance confined,

Yet blessings emerge, in days aligned.

Is this the plan of design.

In this mess of what has become.

CAN'T DEAL WITH LIFE:

I can't deal with life no matter how hard I try.

The only thing I can do is go back to the drink.

Sit there trying to figure what to do next but I can't seem to think.

Confusion seems to play tricks on me

Don't know where I need to be.

I wait for the thunderous storm to come.

While I raise my hands up for the lighting to strike me down.

I'm bleedin, I'm bleedin, with my heart out.

I'm bleedin, I'm bleedin with my soul. I have lived a life of heart ache even though I strive, I have lived for you I have loved you. Oh, heaven please reign down on me. Oh, please look up at me won't, somebody please hear what I have to say.

SHADOWS OF DEEP BETRAYAL'S

I'm angry on the inside no one in my life to show me the light.

I'm on my own everyone I have ever known has betrayed me.

Who is at my side with everything that is in me? I want to run and hide.

In shadows deep, my anger resides,

No guiding light in life to confide.

Alone I stand, in betrayal's embrace,

Lost souls surround, leaving no trace.

Beside me, emptiness, a constant guide,

Yearning to run, in shadows hide.

No solace found, no trust to confide,

In the depths of despair, my emotions abide.

I have never been number one in life no one even knows my name.

I do what I can to shine in my ways that's when I get down to pray.

Life has blasted me not knowing where I'm going to be? I know I'm free in choices that are made.

NOTHING CAME EASY:

I have never been number one in life no one even knows my name.

I do what I can to shine in my ways that's when I get down to pray.

Life has blasted me not knowing, where I'm going to be, but I know I'm free in choices that are made.

People may not know who I am, or where I've been but I know where I have been where I'm going, I'm tired of saying good bye.

Never been given a chance but yet I'm here holdin my stance still alive.

Only God knows where I'm going to be as well as how far I'm gonna go.

No matter if it's a good time or if it's bad.

Time it doesn't matter no how no way.

Nothing has eased the pain, there is no more emotion so now I'm on the wrong side.

I was born into who I am and that's what I know.

CONFUSION REIGNS:

Everything I ever loved has come and gone, always been writing, always been saying what's on my mind, not everyone has been kind. The battles I have been fighting left bruised and batter it’s made me a stronger man, a smarter person.

What is my name again? So much confusion I do not know what is up or down.

In a world where love comes and goes,
I've penned my tales, endured the thrills.
Words on my mind, a relentless stream,
Not all have been kind, life's complex dream.

Battles fought, left bruised and battered,
Yet strength emerged, my spirit unshattered.
A wiser soul, through hardship I've grown,
In this tumultuous journey, I've known.

Confusion reigns, a maze profound,
What's up or down? my name not found.
In the echo of life's mystic sound,
I search for self, lost and then found.

MAKIN THAT DOUGH:

I'm here for the dough now that I'm here I've got to go.

I make no apologies for the money I make.

You don't matter I'm here for the dough now that I've got it; I've got to go.

It's a battle uphill when people talking about you, I'm right back in the sattle with big fat sack on my back making this dough.

While you busy runnin your mouth my pockets are filled up.

Maken everyone around living in a nightmare while they be hating. I be making that paper so why don't you hate me but I'll be making that dough so now that I've got it, I've got to go.

SOLITARY OF SHADOWS:

Can't trust nobody I'm on my own again.

I'm filled with hate, I'm filled with love emotions everywhere I pray. God just get me through this hour because I just do know I'm executed every day.

In the solitary realm of mistrust, where the shadows of isolation loom, I navigate the tumultuous sea of conflicting emotions. A mixture of love and hate swirls within, creating a storm that threatens to drown any sense of serenity. Alone and burdened, I find solace in whispered prayers to a higher power, pleading for strength to endure the relentless execution of my spirit each passing day. Unsure of the road ahead, I cling to the hope that somehow, amidst the chaos, I'll find a path to redemption and a sanctuary for my battered soul.

HURT THE ONES WE LOVE:

We kill the ones we love,

But we invite strangers to beat us.

We abuse the ones we love, we kill the ones we love.

We don't know what we got.

We love strangers, the danger is in the ones we love.

Anticipation comes alongside with surrecticon.

I'm not to be desired,

Mix emotions not going to lie.

Blowing up like tnt going off like a bomb.

There is no settling down the light that once shined has gone dark.

I can't fight this emotion anymore

It hurts when the memories come and play,

Now I'm stuck unable to play.

SWEET SOUL:

Come my sweet soul,

Come my sweet soul,

Come my sweet sweet sweet soul.

There is nothing more to be done.

Come my sweet soul,

No more to be done.

No more pain.

No more neglect or abuse.

No one to amuse let the anger go.

Come and rest my sweet sweet soul,

Most times I could not see the journey has always been dark and lonely.

Wanted to love but others just shoved me to the side.

I was so sacred All's I wanted to do is to hide.

No one loved me.

No one cared for me it was just me with nobody else.

Come my precious child and rest,
Come my genuine child and be protected.
Come and be loved my sweet sweet sweet soul.

LIFE'S TOUGH JOURNEY:

When you don't have opportunities in your life and you strive to do all you can to make it better. Because of where you come from, people tear you down, this world can be cruel and soul crush you. It tears you apart to where you are no longer be alive. The vibrant of the person is on the inside, it also has a way to turn you dark on the inside, to get you into a dark luminous character while clinging to the border side of being grey, dark and cruel with destroying the personality with no reservation. When your vulnerable as child, as you are growing up, you are being brainwashed when you have been told something over and over you believe the lies, as an adult you are living those lies.

In the face of such adversity, it's crucial to remember that resilience can be found in the darkest moments. Despite the challenges and the weight of others' opinions, you have the power to redefine your narrative. Through self-discovery and perseverance, you can break free from the shadows, emerging into a brighter version of yourself, illuminated by your own strength and authenticity. The journey might be tough, but the transformation is worth the fight.

Chapter 8

HOLLOW HEART:

My heart is hollow,
My brain is emptied,
So lost I can't remember where I was at.
All's I know I'm standing with my two feet.
I'm so delusional that defeat is in front of me.
I can't go on I can't do any more.
Everything about me is torn into pieces.
The darkness keeps me company and strange thoughts keeps me warm.
How do I remember anymore?

(Verse 1)
My heart is hollow, my brain is emptied,
Lost in this world where memories have been tempted,
I can't recall where I used to be,
But here I stand, on my own two feet, you see.

(Chorus)

I'm lost and delusional, with defeat before me,
I can't go on, can't take much more, of anything.
Everything about me, torn into pieces it seems,
The darkness is my friend, and strange thoughts in my dreams.

(Verse 2)

How do I remember? How do I find my way?
In this tangled web of night and day,
I search for a light to guide me through,
In this endless struggle, to find what's true.

(Chorus)

I'm lost and delusional, with defeat before me,
I can't go on, can't take much more, of anything.
Everything about me, torn into pieces it seems,
The darkness is my friend, and strange thoughts in my dreams.

(Bridge)

Deep inside, there is no spark,
Im tossed into pieces through the dark,
In the midst of chaos, here is my end

(Chorus)

I'm lost and delusional, with defeat before me,
I can't go on, can't take much more, of anything
Everything about me, torn into pieces it seems,
The darkness is my friend, and strange thoughts in my dreams.

I try to do right:

I don't try to do wrong, but it doesn't matter on which way I go if I do right, or if I do wrong something is always out there to get me because of whom I am.

I do my best is what I have always been told to do, when life gets so crazy so unfortunate, I just want to fold even when I do my best it's still not good enough even when I put my all into it.

What more to do? I have to give in. When I'm given my all what more can I give when I have given enough of everything?

When my world pulled out from underneath me, I'm in a sinking hole that takes me apart.

I have been torn walking down this road.

Living the best that I can, but it seems every day is living in the storm.

(Verse 1)

I try to do right, don't try to do wrong,

But it seems the world's been against me all along,

No matter which way I go, it's a fight so long,

Something's always out there, trying to prove me wrong.

(Chorus)

I do my best, that's what I've always been told,

When life gets crazy and the world feels so cold,

I just want to fold, but I'll be strong and bold,

Even when I give my all, it's still not gold.

(Verse 2)

I'm putting my heart into it, I'm doing my part,

But it feels like I'm fighting against the dark,

What more can I give, I've played my part,

Given enough of everything, from the very start.

(Chorus)

I do my best, that's what I've always been told,
When life gets crazy and the world feels so cold,
I just want to fold, but I'll be strong and bold,
Even when I give my all, it's still not gold.

(Bridge)

When my world's pulled from underneath me,
I'm in a sinking hole, it's plain to see,
But I'll rise again, like a phoenix, free,
No matter what life throws, I'll still believe.

(Chorus)

I do my best, that's what I've always been told,
When life gets crazy and the world feels so cold,
I just want to fold, but I'll be strong and bold,
Even when I give my all, it's still not gold.

HIDING:

I'm tired of hiding of myself doesn't even matter.

Why would you even understand?

You only see one aspect of me

I try to hold it all In.

There are times when I am lost and only want to give up.

But then I remember what I am fighting for what life is worth.

[Verse 1]

I'm tired of hiding, from myself, it seems so absurd,

Why would you even comprehend, my inner world, unheard,

You only see one piece of me, the surface, not the core,

I try to keep it all within, emotions I implore.

[Chorus]

There are times when I am lost, I just want to give it up,

But then I remember what I'm fighting for, life's worth, the cup.

[Verse 2]
In shadows I've been dwelling, in a world so dark and deep,
The secrets that I've been withholding, the promises I keep,
I wear this mask upon my face, a facade for all to see,
But deep inside, I know the truth, the real me, just me.

[Chorus]
There are times when I am lost, I just want to give it up,
But then I remember what I'm fighting for, life's worth, the cup.

[Bridge]
In the darkest of my hours, when the world's too much to bear,
I find strength within my heart, a reason to repair,
I'll rise above the shadows, break through this endless night,
For I know what life is worth, and I'll keep up the fight.

[Chorus]

There are times when I am lost, I just want to give it up,
But then I remember what I'm fighting for, life's worth, the cup.

[Outro]

I'll face the storms that come my way, with courage, I'll survive,
With every step I take, I'll find the will to stay alive,
In this song of inner battles, I've found my melody,
And I'll keep singing it out loud, embracing life so free.

STRUGGLE OF CONFLICT:

Where this is conflict, comes Struggle, where is so, there is a choice to fight that struggle, or to give up and let that win over you, as it takes your life.

Death was at my doorstep reaching to take a hold of me. I didn't know what to do so I picked up a bottle just started to drink not knowing any better but then God came in and said no, no, no, not today are you not taking my son away. So now I have to thank God for my life. I work all day to fulfil the rich man's money only to be left with so little. Only to have a taste of that honey suckle. Barley can tie the buckle on my shoe. A little love in the home without any hope at all the only thing that I know is anger and destruction. That was my environment but now that I have my own family I show as much love as I can while given them dreams to shoot for with lots of love.

TEST OF WILL VERSION I:

(Verse 1)

When your days are dark and dreary,
Hold strong when your eyes are weary.
Remember where you came from,
Never forget how strong you've become.

(Chorus)

Working hard to pay your bills,
With nothing left, it's a test of wills.
Telling your kids it's all okay,
But struggling to find a better way.

(Verse 2)

Alone now, not in the mood,
You kneel to pray, your emotions subdued.
When will it be enough, you wonder,
Feeling like you're torn asunder.

(Chorus)

Walk a mile in my shoes, walk my path,
Struggle like I do, feel the aftermath.
Don't just sit there and preach anew,
All I know is what I know, I'm a man too.

(Bridge)

I'm a father, a brother, an uncle in this land,
Doing the best that I can.
Through the storms and the strife,
I'll navigate this journey called life.

(Chorus)

Working hard to pay our dues,
With hope in our hearts, we won't lose.
Telling our loved ones, "We'll find a way,"
Together we'll face each new day.

TEST OF WILL II VERSION DARK DAYS:

When your days are dark and Drury,

Hold strong when your eyes are weak and old as they become weary.

Remember where you came from and never forgot how strong you are.

Working hard to pay your bills,

With nothing left how do you expect me to stay strong.

Telling my kids everything is OK but have no way to buy food. I'm alone now I'm not in the mood I kneel to pray as my emotions make me cry in place, when is it going to be enough? I don't think I'm tough for my family. Don't you see I got to pretend; so my family don't feel what I feel.

Walk a mile in my shoes work like I work.

Struggle like I struggle then you get to see what is like to be. Don't sit there and preach to me what I need to do.

All's, I know is what I know, I'm a man.

I'm a father, I'm a brother, and an uncle. A man, a dad does the best that he can for his family no matter the struggle, no matter how many tears are shed he never gives up no matter how hard life is.

AFFLICTED PAIN:

(Verse 1)

I breathe deep, I'm in the depths, no return in sight,
My spirit burns with grace and mercy, but I'm trapped in endless night,
Pain afflicts my mind and soul, I feel so disconnected,
This world tore me from who I am, with every ounce of fight respected.

(Pre-Chorus)

Contemplating, collaborating, memorizing my next moves,
You can't imagine how it feels, I want the monster to prove,
Not just to kill, but also to steal, what you don't deserve,
In this world of big dreams, reality's a winding curve.

(Chorus)

This is my life, my life,
This is my life, oh, this is my life,
No one can take this away from me,
In this journey of pain and strife.

(Verse 2)

It never seemed like dreams were real, no helping hand in sight,
My dad, not a man but a distant figure, lost in the night,
Troubles always found their way to me, like a shadow's embrace,
Broken and drowning, taking steps with an ever-furious pace.

(Bridge)

In the kitchen, anger's hold, I couldn't let it go,
It burned inside, a fire untamed, consuming me, you know,
But I'll rise above this darkness, find my way to the light,
In the chaos of my life, I'll reclaim what's right.

(Chorus)

This is my life, my life,
This is my life, oh, this is my life,
No one can take this away from me,
In this journey of pain and strife.

(Outro)

I'll break free from these chains, reclaim my soul's delight,
Though the road is long and steep, I'll find my way to the light,
This is my life, my life, and I won't let it be torn,
I'll rise above the darkness, in my own life, I'll be reborn.

TROUBLE FINDS ME;

I'm breath deep breaths in, I'm in the depths of which there is no return.

My spirit burns with grace and mercy but all there is, is this purely painful afflicted, mind affected spirit, soul deflected.

This world pried me away from being who I am even with every inch of a fight.

Contemplating, collaborating, memorizing.

My next moves you don't know how I feel, I want the monster to come out and play not only to kill but also to steal of what you don't deserve.

Big dreams it really never seemed to be real no one there to help me to understand. I had a dad who was not a man.

Troubles always seemed to find me.

Broken myself, I could be drowning as my steps are taken, with a never ending walk. Standing in the kitchen unless it burned, I couldn't let the anger go, no one had a hold of me in my life.

This is my life, my life,

This is my life,

This is my life, my life,

No one can’t take this away from me.

BLEEDING:

I'm bleedin, I'm bleedin, can't you see me?
My heart's crying out won't you set me free?
Oh, heaven please come and rescue me All's I got left is my soul to plead.

Let me be free of this pain and misery
Ohh please let me free of this pain and misery.

Verse 1:
"In the darkness, I've been lost for so long,
Searching for a place where I belong.
I've faced the storms, the battles, and the strife,
But still, I hold on to this fragile life."

Verse 2:
"With every scar, I've learned to grow,
Through the tears and pain, I've come to know.
Life's a journey, filled with twists and turns,
But in my heart, a flicker of hope still burns."

Verse 3:

"Through the shadows, I've walked this lonely road,
Carrying burdens, a heavy, crushing load.
But I won't surrender, I won't give in,
I'll keep on fighting, searching for a win."

Verse 4:

"As the night falls, and the stars softly gleam,
I'll hold on tighter to my shattered dream.
With each sunrise, I'll find the strength to rise,
In the face of despair, I'll reach for the skies."

TOUCH OF THE TOUCH:

If ya know the good Lord, I pray to him to help me cause once you get around me, I feel your touch I'm just not able to keep my hands off of you; you make me so blue my heart drops onto the floor when you step out that door. You're one the I want you to keep warm tonight come here and let's make that good, good lovin,

Let's not find ourselves in a routine plot but let's us become wild and free in every spot.

SPIRIT TORN:

Wish I could send others to the underworld who won't escape.
Skull is burning, heart is on fire
Spirit torn to pieces.
This person has ceased to exists.
Drained for so long I got used to this.
Everywhere I turn it’s always a burst
I have always been in thirst craving and wanting but knowing It's not there for anyone to care.
My soul has been aching for something that will never be.
I have always thrown gasoline on my flames just so I could survive.
I have been worthless,
I have been touchless,
I have been not wanted for so many years,
That my tears have dried up.
You don't know my pain so let me tell it to you, let you have my mind then you can unfold and unwind.

Can't go into the past to rewind what's the use of being kind. Let's trade shoes to walk mile in my footsteps nothing can get you prepared for what you’re about to witness.

SIMPLIFIED:

**Verse 1: **

Simplefie my motto, the way I choose to live,
In this unpredictable world, take what it may give,
Today's a mystery, tomorrow's an open page,
Why overthink it? Let's share a drink and engage,
What am I inviting into this life of mine,
Tonight, under the moon's glow, everything feels fine.

**Chorus: **

So, let's raise a glass together, all good friends unite,
Let our worries scatter, under the starry night.

**Verse 2: **

With friends all around, we're on thc brink,
Of a night so memorable, that's what we all think,
Let's craft a tale with words, a story we'll create,
With every laughter and cheer, we'll celebrate,
What am I welcoming into my world so wide,
Dancing to my heart's rhythm, let's enjoy the ride.

**Chorus: **

What today might bring, or tomorrow might sing,

Let's groove to our own beat, let our spirits take wing,

Raise a glass to life's moments, both big and slight,

Under the moon's soft glow, we'll be alright.

CYCLE BREAKING ME:

Ding doing knock knock
Guess who it is?
Guess who this is?
you know what it is?
what it is not.
Walking around dreaming clowning around unchecked,
un-challenged
I managed to get this far.
Even though I'm living in doubt,
Walking around trying to figure it out
There is no help to be found.
So I go back to the only thing that I have ever known
straight back to the addiction but I can't even have any
kind of admission to myself cause it eases the pain that is
so real so I don't have to feel.
Tired of putting up this fight,
Tired of all of these sleepless nights.

And it just keeps spinning around, around, and around, I do what I can to break the cycle but the cycle breaks me
So I have gone.
back to pills and the drink.

PUSHING BOUNDARIES:

(Verse 1)

I've always been that soul,

Pushing boundaries, losing control.

One foot off the ledge, daring fate,

While the other's on the ground, it's a balancing state.

(Chorus)

Leaning towards the edge, more than on the ground,

A little push could make my world spin 'round.

Heart pounding, surrounded by empty space,

Never satisfied, in this relentless chase.

(Verse 2)

Isolation calls, a desire so strong,

Away from the crowd, where I truly belong.

Rain pouring down, where do I go?

No one to comfort, just myself in the flow.

(Chorus)

Leaning towards the edge, more than on the ground,
A little push could make my world spin 'round.
Heart pounding, surrounded by empty space,
Never satisfied, in this relentless chase.

(Bridge)

Wind blowing hard, am I being blown away?
Seeking solace, where shadows play.
Nothing to show, in this relentless storm,
Yet, I stand firm, embracing the norm.

(Verse 3)

I crave the silence, away from the noise,
A solitary journey, my soul deploys.
In the rain, I find my own shelter,
Lost in thoughts, a lone helter-skelter.

(Chorus)

Leaning towards the edge, more than on the ground,
A little push could make my world spin 'round.
Heart pounding, surrounded by empty space,
Never satisfied, in this relentless chase.

(Outro)

When the rain is pouring, and the wind blows strong,
I'll find my way, where I truly belong.
No need for comfort, no need to show,
Just myself and I, in the afterglow.

Fight the pain God will show up:

(Verse 1)

In a world where conflict thrives,
Struggles come and steal our lives.
We face a choice, to fight the pain,
Or let it win, in our hearts, it stains.

(Pre-Chorus)

Death was knocking, at my door,
I reached for a bottle, unsure what's in store.
But then God's voice, it filled the air,
Said, "Not today, my child, I'm here to care."

(Chorus)

So, I thank God for my life,
Though I work all day, face endless struggles.
Chasing riches, left with so little,
But with love and dreams, my heart can fiddle.

(Verse 2)

Like honey suckle, life can be sweet,
But the world can knock you off your feet.
Anger and destruction, my past did sow,
But now I've got my family, and love to show.

(Bridge)

I'll give them dreams to chase so high,
With love, hope, and the endless sky.
No more anger, no more despair,
In this life, together, we'll make it fair.

(Chorus)

So, I thank God for my life,
Though I work all day, face endless strife.
Chasing riches, left with so little,
But with love and dreams, my heart can fiddle.

Chapter 9

DARK ROAD GRINDING:

I go to bed in the dark, I wake up in the dark, I grind and grind only to beat my head against a Brick wall til I start to bleed.

I am hollow,

I am empty no one hears me,

I am on a dark road with wight gripping me.

Waiting, wanting to crash, to break, to burn.

I had dreams but they quickly got ripped away from me I thought I knew what I wanted but I don't know anymore.

I just hear the Crow squawking in my head and I hear nothing else.

I just want to end it all I can't cope.

I can't deal no matter how strong I am.

I got what I wanted but I'm not happy.

FUCKED CHARISMATIC MAN:

I'm a fucked up charismatic man.

Who wants what he can't have,

Work hard for everything only to end up having very little of nothing.

Been unattractive to everyone around me.

In shadows of self, a charismatic flaw,

Yearning for what's out of grasp, an unmet draw.

Toilsome efforts, fruits of labor thin,

A life of little, where nothing seems to win.

Unattractive echoes in the crowd's gaze,

Yet resilient heart navigates life's maze.

Charisma and flaws entwined, a complex dance,

Seeking solace in a world's fleeting glance.

DON'T KNOW IF IM GOING TO MAKE IT:

Tell them I say hello,

I don't know if I am going to make it,

I look forward on the outside faking it but on the inside,

I'm blowing up.

Depression hits my mind,

The anger I feel inside.

Disappointment is in my soul.

How did I let my life become like this

All's I do is my hardest.

I feel defeated cause I can't make ends meet. My children see me working hard.

They don't see the struggle that we go through. I sit back and think to myself how am I going to make it this week? As I am in defeat it's hard and the days seem to be getting darker and darker even though I wish for a clear day. Is my mind, right? Everyday seems to be a battle of surviving. Some days I want to give in and give up I don't know whom I going to talk to last, but is this the day that is my last day here?

SONG TO THE POEM DONT KNOW IF IM GOING TO MAKE IT;

DEPRESSION GRIPS MY MIND:

(Verse 1)

Tell them I say hello, as I walk through the storm,
I don't know if I'll make it, but I'll transform,
I wear a fake smile, but inside, I'm torn,
Depression grips my mind, like a thorny thorn.

(Chorus)

I'm fighting this anger deep within my soul,
Disappointment's taken hold, it's taken its toll,
How did I let my life, take such a heavy toll?
I give it my all, but it's still an uphill goal.

(Verse 2)

I feel defeated, struggling to make ends meet,
My children see me working, but they're unaware, so sweet,
They don't see the battles, the struggles that we keep,
I wonder how I'll make it this week, it's no easy feat.

(Chorus)

I'm fighting this anger deep within my soul,
Disappointment's taken hold, it's taken its toll,
How did I let my life, take such a heavy toll?
I give it my all, but it's still an uphill goal.

(Bridge)

In the darkness of my days, I'm searching for the light,
Hoping for a clear day to end this endless fight,
Is my mind, right? Will I make it through the night?
Every day's a battle, just trying to survive.

(Verse 3)

Some days I want to give in, to surrender and resign,
I don't know who I'll talk to last, in this troubled mind,
But every day's a chance to find a way to climb,
I'll keep on pushing forward, leaving the past behind.

(Chorus)

I'm fighting this anger deep within my soul,
Disappointment's taken hold, it's taken its toll,
How did I let my life, take such a heavy toll?
I give it my all, but it's still an uphill goal.

(Outro)

Tell them I say hello, as I stand strong and tall,
I'll keep fighting through the darkness, breaking down the wall,
Though the road is tough, I won't let myself fall,
In this song of my life, I'll rise above it all.

NOTHING LEFT:

Why do you drain my energy away?
Why do I let you take it, day by day?
Why did I open up, let you inside,
When all you do is leave me far and wide?

I've got nothing left to give, can't you see,
You come to me, but it's all about you
I just want to see you lie there as you are dying, and I don't care,
You were never there, left me in despair.

No energy left, it's running dry,
You were there to watch me, then to say goodbye.
I was all alone when I needed a hand,
You left me to my fate, I don't understand.

You weren't there when I needed a father,
Left me in the darkness, alone to descend.

Now I've realized, I'm better off without you,

No more wasted energy.

GLEAMING OF PASSION:

The gleam in your eyes when I see you,
Makes me smile you are beaming light.
In your soul.
In your gaze, a radiant gleam so true,
A smile blooms, your light breaks through.
Within your soul, a radiant beam,
The joy in your eyes, a love supreme.
We embrace as our bodies are deemed into one another as the stars dance around us as we unburden ourselves. As we let our bodies dance into each other with passion of ease for joy to be fulfilled as our souls are emerge together never departing.
In the luminescent depths of your gaze,
A radiant gleam, a love ablaze.
Smiles bloom like petals in the night,
You're the beacon, casting out the light.

Our bodies entwine, a cosmic waltz,
Stars bear witness, our connection exalts.
Unburdened souls in this cosmic trance,

Dancing together, a passionate advance.

As celestial bodies pirouette,
Our essence merges, an eternal duet.
Joy fulfilled, a dance of souls untold,
Together, entwined, a story unfolds.

LIFE'S GRIND:

I can't wait til it's all said and done

Where I have gone,

No one will know,

This life had a grind on me,

Til I had no mind at all.

It's only when it's time to fall is when you know who's in your life.

But even then, I am broken,

I am not able to go back again.

My eyes lay before me.

I cannot stand being me.

I wish I was someone else.

My dreams, my life has been broken.

So confused I don't even know how too infuse my worth into society.

So, I decided not to have any sobriety. I don't even know the answers. My life has been but nothing, it has been lies so why even try to fight? My hands have always been tied. I wanna break away but I don't how.

STATE TO STAE:

Hi I'm Kevin I'm from Idaho moved to Arizona.

In Idaho's land of mountains high I stood,

With dreams and hopes, my heart felt good.

But destiny called, and I set my sight,

On Arizona's desert, where the sun shines bright.

From the Gem State's charm to cacti tall,

I journeyed far, leaving it all.

Kevin's the name, and here I reside,

In Arizona's warmth, where dreams collide.

The landscapes change, but the spirit remains,

In the Southwest sun, where adventure gains.

Idaho's memories, Arizona's embrace,

Two worlds combined in this life's chase.

SERPENTS DEEP VENOMOUS BITE:

I feel the snake bite as the venom runs through my blood.
I lay there in the night,
In shadows deep, the serpent's fang did pierce,
A venomous dance through my veins, fierce.
Beneath the moon's muted, silent light,
I lay embraced by the venom's bite.
Vexation is in my lips kiss of death is what is to be.
Raised in toxicity now I live in it only to survive. I bite first so I don't get betrayed, now you lay in your head to rest, no more solace, no more noise as I stand there as being poised.
Beneath the veil of night's obsidian shroud,
A serpent's bite, a dance, venom endowed.
Through veins it courses, fierce and free,
Moon's silent witness to the agony.

Vexation echoes in each whispered breath,
A kiss of death lingers, a dance with death.

Raised in toxicity's cruel embrace,
Now living within it, a relentless chase.

Survival's mantra, a bite as shield,
In shadows, trust betrayed, scars concealed.
As you rest, solace fades away,
Silence reigns, poised in the night's ballet.

THE DAY IS KILLING ME:

(Verse 1)

Shoot me down, cut me up, and take me to the edge,
Every day's a nightmare, can't escape what's in my head,
Never learned to be happy, I'm always raging deep within,
Holding it until I burst, then they say I've lost my spin.

(Pre-Chorus)

But they don't know my journey, they don't owe me a thing,
I just wanna live my life, without all the strings,
People are so shrewd, they'll screw you if they can,
Excuse me if I'm rude, it's just the way I am.

(Chorus)

I'm nice until life pushes me to the brink,
Then I lose control, it's like I'm on the brink,
So, sit back, relax, enjoy this tale unfold,
This is who I am, let my story be told.

(Verse 2)

I've been through the battles, seen the darkest of nights,
Fighting through the shadows, where demons take their flights,
But I won't be a victim, I won't just fade away,
I'll stand up to the challenge, come what may.

(Pre-Chorus)

They don't know my journey, they don't owe me a thing,
I just wanna live my life, without all the strings,
People are so shrewd, they'll screw you if they can,
Excuse me if I'm rude, it's just the way I am.

(Chorus)

I'm nice until life pushes me to the brink,
Then I lose control, it's like I'm on the brink,
So, sit back, relax, enjoy this tale unfold,
This is who I am, let my story be told.

(Bridge)

In this rock 'n' roll story, I'll stand my ground,
The darkness won't control me, I won't be bound,
I'll rise from the ashes, a phoenix from the fire,
My spirit's burning brighter, reaching higher and higher.

(Chorus)

I'm nice until life pushes me to the brink,
Then I lose control, it's like I'm on the brink,
So, sit back, relax, enjoy this tale unfold,
This is who I am, let my story be told.

(Outro)

Now you've seen my journey, the battles I've faced,
The strength that's within me, can't be erased,
I'll keep on rockin', through the highs and the lows,
This is my story, and it's the way it goes.

Living A Angry Nightmare:

Just shoot me down cut me up and fucking kill me.

Every day is a living nightmare for me.

Never learned how to be happy always angry on the inside I hold it in till I Burst out look to see what people say I'm crazy where does he belong?

But they don't know me,

They don't owe me just want to live my life.

With out being screwed people are just so shrewd so excuse if I am being fucking rude. I am nice until Life pushes me to the edge then I fucking loose control.

So, sit back relax enjoy watching this show unfold cause this who I am for my story to be told.

MY SHADOWS DEEP:

In shadows deep, I lay to rest,
A life in darkness, pain's cruel jest.
Each day I grind, my spirit's spark,
Against a wall, I'm torn apart.

My soul, a void, an empty space,
No solace found, no saving grace.
In silence, I cry, but no one hears,
I'm drowning in my haunting fears.

On this dark road, a weight I bear,
Craving to shatter, to break, to tear.
Dreams once held, now torn and frayed,
I'm lost, confused, my path decayed.

The crow's harsh caw within my mind,
A torment, cruel, no peace to find.
I yearn for release, to end the strife,

To escape this never-ending, bleak life.
I thought I knew what happiness meant,

But now I'm trapped, in discontent.
I long for solace, for a way to cope,
But in this abyss, there's little hope.

SHADOWS CAST OF BEING ALONE:

My roots have not been deepened of where I was supposed to be.

As child growing into man, I was robbed of what life was supposed to be.

There was no glee in the eye only disruption of no stability.

No father to teach me, so I had to learn my own way no teacher would stay by me but instead I was told I wasn't good enough go over there and be a tree in the play.

Tossed into the wind with disarray

Who would take me in? Only the wind is at my presence while the leaves blow at my feet as the sun keeps me warm even in the dead of winter I am alone.

Who will take me in?

Why am I always so alone?

There is no home.

As my feet allow me to roam.

In shadows cast, my roots, they weep and ache,

No place to call my own, a life forsaken.

As youth, I yearned for joys I'd never taste,
A world of constant chaos, not a haven.

No father's guiding hand, no lessons learned,
I charted lonely paths, no light to see.
A tree in the play, I stood, undiscerned,
With whispered words, they deemed me not to be.

Tossed like leaves in the wind's relentless sway,
A wanderer, with disarray, I tread.
No shelter found, just sun's deceptive ray,
In winter's grasp, I roam, my heart like lead.

Who takes me in, and ends this ceaseless roam?
In solitude, I dwell, no place called home.

POOR MAN LIVING:

(Verse 1)
I ain't got my money right, it's a constant uphill climb,
Bills are due, but payday's far, just two more weeks in time,
Every day's a struggle, living on a shoestring so tight,
Broke as hell, it feels like life's a never-ending fight.

(Chorus)
No gas, no cash, no food for the kids,
I'm working ten days straight, no time to hit the skids,
Three jobs, no days off, it's a brutal grind,
Credit scores in the gutter, life's unkind.

(Verse 2)
No plates to eat on, no car to drive around,
Stuck in this cycle, it's got me feeling bound,
Always in the negative, it's tough to rise above,
One bill paid, another's lurking, the struggle's real, my love.

(Chorus)

No gas, no cash, no food for the kids,
I'm working ten days straight, no time to hit the skids,
Three jobs, no days off, it's a brutal grind,
Credit scores in the gutter, life's unkind.

(Bridge)

But I keep on pushing, gotta find a way,
To break this cycle, make a brighter day,
I'll keep on fighting, can't give up this fight,
I'll find a path to make my future bright.

(Chorus)

No gas, no cash, no food for the kids,
I'm working ten days straight, no time to hit
the skids,
Three jobs, no days off, it's a brutal grind,
Credit score's in the gutter, life's unkind.

(Outro)

I'll rise above this struggle, find a way to cope,
Though the road is tough, I won't give up hope,
Life's a battle, but I'll stand tall and strong,
Sing this song of resilience, and prove them all wrong.

Chapter 10

<u>DESTRUCTION DANCES:</u>

(Verse 1)

Destruction danced into my life, played its part,
Taught me survival, etched it in my heart.
Lost and confused, somehow, I held my ground,
In the echoes of destruction, resilience profound.

(Chorus)

Survival's melody, a song in my heart,
A symphony of resilience, a work of art.
Life constructed me, a lesson to impart,
Grateful day by day, one step at a start.

(Verse 2)

I don't know how I've held it together,
Through storms and shadows, in any weather.
Learning from mistakes, in life's grand design,
I can’t be living One day at a time, resilience refined.

(Chorus)

Survival's melody, a song in my heart,
A symphony of resilience, a work of art.
Life constructed me, a lesson to impart,
Grateful day by day, one step at a start.

(Bridge)

In the rhythm of chaos, I found my grace,
Each trial and error, a chapter to embrace.
Destruction's echoes, a teacher so wise,
In the school of life, where the resilient rise.

(Verse 3)

Life has crafted me, shaped my destiny,
A journey of growth, a profound legacy.
Take it one day at a time, the mantra I've known,
In the dance of destruction, resilience has grown.

(Chorus)

Survival's melody, a song in my heart,
A symphony of resilience, a work of art.
Life constructed me, a lesson to impart,
Grateful day by day, one step at a start.

(Outro)

So let the echoes fade, in the rearview of time,
A tapestry of resilience, a life so sublime.
Through destruction's symphony, I found my rhyme,
Grateful for each lesson, in this life of mine.

DESTRUCTION TEACHES:

Destruction has come in so many ways into life, it teaches you too stand strong:

You learned what you are made of. Destruction is a construct of being a teacher as it teaches you too rebuild what has been torn down. Destruction shows you what kind of a mind you have as a person. You are as if you Wither away shows you a type of person that can learn, that can rebuild, to be a leader, how to solve problems. Even when you don't see the answer that is in front of you. Destruction that has played a part in your life will show you who people truly are. Are they going to help you? Are they going to stand by your side? Or are they going to look at you look at the mess as they don't move in to help? Only talk about what needs to be done and do nothing. Or are they the type that say nothing, who sees what needs to be done, knows how to help they just jump in to help without saying a word. DESTRUCTION is an implemented tool that God has used over and over again.

PARANOIA:

Always think someone is out to get me,

People have always been put off by me, but yet they refuse to get to know me and instead they put me in categories, as they judge me. That's why I stay silent and let my words be read, if you know me you wouldn't judge me, if you talked to me then you would see another side, but instead you condemn me, you throw me out, you put slanderous words to my name. You have no idea what I've been through but yet I am standing here I've muddle through the struggle of my childhood now that I have my own kids, I'm hoping they don't feel the same.

VAST PLAINS:

Upon vast plains where grass stands tall,
My knees embraced by its verdant sprawl.
Soft wind whispers against my skin,
Through my hair, a gentle, rhythmic spin.

Gushing sounds, a nature's song,
As the tree tips, in green, belong.
Splendid mountains on the horizon rise,
Under storm clouds, painting gray skies.

Roar of thunder, a mighty sound,
Crashing through the plains, echoes abound.
I stand, still, gazing upward wide,
Breathing deeply, the world as my guide.

In this moment, nature's grand display,
Yet, amid beauty, a shadow's fray.
The grim reaper roams with silent tread,
In black monk robe, his presence spread.

Sickle in hand, he hovers nearby,
Through fields and plains, devoid of fear.
I run, heart pounding, a desperate flight,
Not ready to yield to eternal night.

Amid confusion, I question fate,
Dream or reality, a blurred state.
Where am I, between heaven and hell?
Death lingers, a tale hard to tell.

Time races, questions fill the air,
Why does death pursue, why does he dare?
Is my time up, the answers unclear,
In this realm, a blend of hope and fear.

UN-MET NEEDS:

I'm not a good guy but I'm not a villain either living in this life I wish I had super powers. Each day has been a challenge gave it my all. Lost everything I've had, now I don't have nothing to lose.

In the shadows I reside, neither saint nor fiend,
Dreaming of powers, a life's unmet need.
Every day, a struggle, a relentless test,
Gave my all, yet lost, in this life's quest.

Once possessed it all, now nothing to cling,
A journey of loss, like a broken wing.
No hero, no villain, just a soul laid bare,
In the void of nothingness, I find solace there.

HURT OF A CHILD:

I’m hurting, I'm trying.

Feeling sad don't know how long I can go on with this pace.

I have fallen far from grace,

Wish I could go back to the childhood times to familiar faces.

So much going on I don't know how to handle it all turned into a deep depression.

I'm so hard pressed I don't know how to carry on anymore.

Running down the road trying to out run the hurt and pain.

I think it's time for a little drink.

Go around the corner to hide it all

Shoot up, drink up, run from it all,

I just need another day to pull it together hold on just a little bit longer another sip from the bottle.

BENEATH THE COLD ICE:

Cold as Ice black is dark,

This Life has me in a vice grip

Shivering as I'm quivering,

I try to get away from the grip that this life has on me there is nowhere to run.

The small voice in my head says I'm done, No more breathing, no more life.

Everything has been fort fit.

Life has finally caught up with me bruised and battered. I have been nothing more than defeat, now as I lay on the ground with my cold feet what is to be next? As others minds are per placed of what has happened. Left this world now am I finally at peace?

Beneath the ice, cold as ice, black is dark in shadows stark,

Life's vice grips me, cold and dark.

Shivering, quivering, I strive to flee,

But life's relentless hold won't set me free.

No refuge found, nowhere to run,

A whispered voice declares I'm done.
No more breath, no more life gone in a glance.
All forfeited, in a defeated state of being in a trance.

Bruised and battered, I lie in defeat,
Cold feet on the ground, life's bitter feat.
What's next in this perplexing quest?
Have I found peace, am I finally at rest?

A MOMENTS SHADWOS CAST:

In a tumultuous realm where chaos unfolds,
I find myself lost; my story untold.
Out of control, in life's tangled maze,
No solutions in sight, just a daunting haze.

Promised a better life, a vow from the past,
Now I reflect on missteps, shadows cast.
Frustration grips tight, like a vice on my soul,
Lost in the echoes of a broken life's toll.

Praying for change in this moment today,
Yet hanging by a thread, emotions at bay.
Contemplating a leap from a rooftop so high,
But what of the echoes, the unanswered why?

In the abyss of despair, where can I find,
A glimmer of hope, a saving kind?
For I am a thread away from the fall,

Seeking a lifeline, a cure for it all.

The Devil has been playing with my mind using his tricks on me to see if I would slip up getting me off of focus from God, blockade are along with obstacles in my way to see if I would come to him luring me away to see if I would stay but I knew how to pray.

LOOKING FAMILIAR:

You look familiar please don't pull that trigger you don't remember seeing each other?

All’s you need to do is to look in the mirror that is on the wall then you will see the memories, memories will bring you back to life so no need to cry anymore it’s just the way you are.

You been near but yet so Far. You got in the car and drove away never to be seen or heard of again.

I was left alone standing there with tears to my eyes left in the dark with the street lights on and every one was gone.

I faded away into the cloudy midnight dark night.

I was cold and shivering I was trying to stay warm with all of my might. I had no one near, so I could not live one day at time. All’s I had to keep me company was my own fear.

In the shadows of a distant past,
You seem familiar, a moment cast.
Hold back that trigger, don't let it ignite,
For in this reflection, memories alight.

A mirror on the wall, a portal to the past,
Look deep within, let the echoes last.
No need to weep, the truth is near,
You're more than a ghost, dispel that fear.

Once so close, now distantly apart,
In a car, you departed, a vanishing art.
Alone I stood, tears in the night,
Street lights flickered, all out of sight.

Fade into the midnight, a cloudy embrace,
Cold and shivering in that lonesome space.
No one to warm, no one to hold,
Only my fears, a story to be told.

SONG TO THE POEM LOOKING FAMILIAR:

(Verse 1)

In the shadows of a memory, you seem so nearby,

But don't pull that trigger, let the past reappear.

Look in the mirror, hanging on the wall,

See the reflections, the memories enthral.

(Chorus)

No need to cry, it's just the way you are,

Once so close, now distant, like a fading star.

You got in the car, drove away so far,

Left me standing alone, under the streetlight's scar.

(Verse 2)

In the cloudy midnight, I faded away,

Left in the dark, where everyone went astray.

Cold and shivering, trying to stay warm,

One day at a time, facing fears, weathering the storm.

(Bridge)

You were once near, but now so far,
A silent departure, like a falling star.
The echoes of your absence, haunting the night,
I stood alone, left with tears and the streetlight.

(Chorus)

No need to cry, it's just the way you are,
Once so close, now distant, like a fading star.
You got in the car, drove away so far,
Left me standing alone, under the streetlight's scar.

(Outro)

As the memories linger, I'll find my way,
Living one day at a time, in the light of the day.
No one near, just my own fear,
But I'll keep going, shedding the midnight tear.

CAN'T ESCAPE THE FIGHT:

(Verse 1)

I've given my all, did my best,

Fighting each day, but now I need to rest.

Beaten down, I'm at the end of the quest,

It's time to say goodbye, put my troubles to rest.

(Chorus)

I've fought and fought with the same thought,

Is it worth it today, or have I lost the lot?

Can't escape myself, stuck in my own head,

Down this road again, where the torment is bred.

(Verse 2)

Waking up each day, same old fight,

Wondering if it's worth it, in the fading light.

Can't stand who I am, trapped in my own despair,

Been down this road before, life isn't

always fair.

(Chorus)
I've fought and fought with the same thought,
Is it worth it today, or have I lost the lot?
Can't escape myself, stuck in my own head,
Down this road again, where the torment is bred.

(Bridge)
Dark grey haze, another day,
People fear me, but they don't know the way.
Running away, everyone and everything,
In this lonely space, where I'm left to cling.

(Verse 3)
The walls close in, reaching out to take,
Back into the torment, every step I make.
Reality blurs, emotions become a chore,
Just another day, in this dark gray lore.

(Chorus)

I've fought and fought with the same thought,
Is it worth it today, or have I lost the lot?
Can't escape myself, stuck in my own head,
Down this road again, where the torment is bred.

(Outro)

But maybe there's hope, a flicker in the night,
A chance to break free, to see a different light.
So here I stand, at the crossroads in dismay,
Hoping for a change, a brighter, sunnier day.

FIGHTING THE DAY:

I have really tried to do my best.

I gave it my all of what I got. But now I'm so beaten down all there is left to do is to say goodbye.

I have fought and fought waking every day with the same thought.

How am I going to make it? Is it worth fighting today before I lose it all?

Can't stand myself can't get out of my own head I have been here before.

Down this road here we go again the walls reach out to grab me back in the torment. It is so real but I can't feel anything anymore, just another day that is a dark grey haze. People are scared of me but fail to get to know mc, everyone and everything runs away from me.

JOY'S UN-FOLDS:

It's the small things in life we all enjoy to see and watch. It's fulling to hear a child's laughter. Going through life struggling to keep going, into the mud like a cow. Chewing up cud moving from one town to another living in the country to seeing the city life but the country life is for me. I miss the smell of the country tree hills seeing the snow top mountains yes sir the country life is for me.

THE STRUGGLE KEEPS GETTING HARDER:

(Verse 1)

Each day, it's a struggle, getting harder and harder,
Facing life feels impossible; it's a heavy carder.
I rise, hoping for change, but failure is my guide,
Doors slammed in my face; every effort denied.

(Chorus)

I carry my head low, defeated and bruised,
Life's winning, and I feel like I've lost and been used.
My mind's a whirlwind, my world's a coaster,
Can't express what I need, it's a verbal imposter.

(Verse 2)

Words elude me, like shadows in the dark,
Left with nothing but a prayer, a feeble spark.
My mind weighs heavy, my heart's burdened too,
Strayed far away, standing alone, feeling askew.

(Chorus)

I kneel and pray, as my strength slips away,
Might is gone, weakness here to stay.
Nothing left to say, just goodbye to the day,
Eyes closing shut, I fade, and I sway.

(Bridge)

In this roller coaster life, I've become weak,
Lost in the whirlwind, the future looks bleak.
Stranded alone, with nothing in sight,
I'm left here standing, fading into the night.

(Verse 3)

I'm adrift, far from where I used to be,
Silent goodbyes, as my soul sets free.
No answers, just questions, in this endless maze,
Lost in the echoes of life's perplexing phase.

(Chorus)

My mind and heart, a heavy blend,
Struggling alone, with no one to defend.
I don't understand, as I close my eyes tight,
Fading away, into the silent night.

STRUGGLING TO COPE:

In shadows I lie, bedtime's dark embrace,
Awakening to shadows, in a relentless chase.
Grinding, striving, against a wall of stone,
Bleeding, I'm hollow, in solitude I moan.

A desolate road, with a weight so profound,
Craving collision, to break, to be unbound.
Dreams snatched away, like leaves in the wind,
Lost on a journey, where confusion is thinned.

The echoes of a crow, a relentless caw,
Deafening silence, an unforgiving draw.
Yearning for peace, as emotions elope,
In the vast emptiness, a soul without hope.

I obtained my desires, yet joy is a stranger,
Strength wanes, in the face of inner danger.
Struggling to cope, unable to endure,

In this somber landscape, pain is pure.
Yet, hold on dear spirit, let solace find its way,
For tomorrow may bring the light of a new day.

Each day keeps getting harder and harder.
Barely can face the day how do you expect me to face life? I get up trying to make a change but I fail each time. I even try with every door shut in my face and slammed in front of me. I carry my head down low feel so defeated, feel like that life is winning and I am loosing. I feel like my mind is in a whirlwind my world is a roller coaster.
I don't get out what I need to say
All there is left to do is to kneel and pray.
My mind weighs, my heart. My heart is heavy, I don't understand it now that I have strayed far away, I'm left here standing alone with nothing in sight. I have become weak now that my might is gone, I have nothing left to say except good bye to this day as my eyes close shut.

Chapter 11

QUESTIONS ABOUT DEATH:

What does death mean?

What does life mean?

What is the heart of Man?

Even if it means that we do all we can for those around us.

A lot of us fall through the Crack as our voices are never heard.

Our echoes fall silent as others around us become violent.

Our footprint is erased as hypocrisy covers with deceit.

When it's all said and done do we really lie in the ground and be at peace?

Did I do enough or lasted long enough?

For those who mourned let the truth lie on the table and let your hearts be seeing for what you are and what your life is.

Let this message be done either your heart will hear or this will fall on the unwise of deaf ears.

STRIVING TO FIGHT:

(Verse 1)

In the shadows, my life's always spun,
Heart ablaze, while others come undone.
Apart from the crowd, beneath the stars I pray,
Memories cut deep, tears in my soul portray.

(Chorus)

Taking my best shot, facing knives in the back,
Yet I try, though it feels like an endless track.
Don't know why I strive, feeling so out of sync,
Fighting myself, trying hard not to sink.

(Verse 2)

Hurt locker trips, time after time,
Emotional scars, like a relentless climb.
Told not to express, but I break the mould,
Dreaming the impossible when everything's cold.

(Bridge)

Billions dream, don't let it all shut down,
In the silence, unseen doors abound.
Your dreams, your reality, let them unfold,
Gravitate to success, let your story be told.

(Chorus)

Always keep going, in the face of despair,
Fight for your life, it's yours to declare.
You can decide, to give up or rise,
Elevate yourself to the next, beyond the skies.

(Verse 3)

Told I'd be a nobody, but God intervened,
Opened doors, a path of achievement keen.
Keep on fighting, never surrender the fight,
Your dreams, your beacon, guiding through the night.

(Outro)

Always keep pushing, don't heed what they say,
In the face of challenges, find your own way.
Rise above the tales you've been told,
Elevate to the next level, let your story unfold.

PAINFUL MEMORIES:

My life has always been in the shadows.

With a fire in my heart,

While everybody else is apart from,

Praying underneath the stars.

Too many painful memories that leaves tears in my soul with so many emotional scars.

I take my best shot at life but too many knives in the back.

I don't know why I even try.

Killing myself just trying to make it,

Time after time the hurt locker comes and trips me up.

I have been told not to express myself,

Think Billions, dream the impossible, when everything is shut down on you don't give up, know that the unseen doors are opening, your dreams are your reality. I gravitate into success where I was told you will be a nobody. God opened the doors to the path of achievement.

Always keep going,

Always keep fighting it's your life you can decide to give up or raise above what you been told, be elevated to the next level.

CHAOTIC LOSS:

(Verse 1)

I'm a man stuck, in the struggle, it's my daily ride,
Told I'd go nowhere, but that won't be my guide.
Life's angles suffocate, feels like I'm bound,
In this chaotic mess, losing, but I won't back down.

(Pre-Chorus)

Living daily, choices made on a guess,
Right or wrong, it's all just a mess.
Doesn't matter what you've done or how hard you strive,
Judged by the wrongs, that's how we survive.

(Chorus)

Come at me, I'm not afraid to speak my mind,
I know my past, my strength, you'll find.
With faults and all, I stand strong and true,
Nothing more you can do; I'll see it through.

(Verse 2)

Struggling daily, but I'm breaking free,
Against the odds, I'll find my decree.
In the chaos, I'll carve my own way,
No fear, no regrets, it's my time to sway.

(Pre-Chorus)

Living daily, choices made on a guess,
Right or wrong, it's all just a mess.
Doesn't matter what you've done or how hard you strive,
Judged by the wrongs, that's how we survive.

(Chorus)

Come at me, I'm not afraid to speak my mind,
I know my past, my strength, you'll find.
With faults and all, I stand strong and true,
Nothing more you can do; I'll see it through.

(Bridge)

I'll rise above, in the face of the storm,
Every mistake, a lesson to inform.
Through the struggle, I'll find my way,
I'm not afraid, I've got more to say.

(Chorus)

Come at me, I'm not afraid to speak my mind,
I know my past, my strength, you'll find.
With faults and all, I stand strong and true,
Nothing more you can do; I'll see it through.

(Outro)

So here I am, in the midst of the fight,
I'll own my story, in the dark or in the light.
No more fear, no more to prove,
I'll be remembered for the life I choose.

SEARCHING FOR A WAY:

(Verse 1)

In the maze of life, I'm searching for a way,

Stuck around the corner, can't see the light of day.

Persisting daily, when life hits its low,

A whisper in my mind says, "One more step to go."

(Pre-Chorus)

It's not a marathon, but a race against time,

Learning to get things right, a rhythm, a rhyme.

Things may seem tight, the struggles so real,

Believe in yourself, that's the magic appeal.

(Chorus)

Give me one more inch, give me one more step,

One more effort, keep going, don't forget.

This journey's tough, but you can make it through,

Believe in yourself, the power is in you.

(Verse 2)

Telling stories of battles, both lost and won,
Memories, a burden, heavy like the sun.
Flashbacks haunt me, emotions on display,
Thanking God for grace, guiding me each day.

(Bridge)

From a torn family, nowhere to climb,
Left to drown, in the waves of time.
But I rise above, with strength profound,
Turn the page, a new chapter found.

(Chorus)

Give me one more inch, give me one more step,
One more effort, keep going, don't forget.
This journey's tough, but you can make it through,
Believe in yourself, the power is in you.

(Outro)

No longer carrying the burdens of the past,
I'm free from the shadows that were cast.
With faith in myself and grace from above,
I conquer the journey, with strength and love.

ONE MORE STEP:

Just trying to figure out the right formula too get around the corner I seem to be stuck and can't get around this bend. I keep on keeping on with persistence on a daily basis even when life seems to be at the lowest. You can't seem to go on, it's that little voice in your head saying come on give me one more inch, give me one more step, give me one more effort, keep going one more time this is not a marathon race this a race of time and to learn to get things right.

I know things are really tight but you can do this, you can make it All's you have to do is to believe in yourself. No matter how hard things get or what you lose. I need to tell my stories of my battles that I have fought lost and won. The memories that I carry is a burden I can no longer carry and I'm done.

Emotions engulf me when I have flashbacks of what took place I can only thank God for his savings grace. I come from a torn family with nowhere to go to, a mountain to climb but I was left only to drown in my own mind.

WAGES:

(Verse 1)

In a world where wages are low, costs reach the sky,
Corporate greed thrives, pockets lined up high.
Locals outsourced, forced to the streets,
Homeless populations, bruised and beaten, it repeats.

(Chorus)

How did I not listen, now I'm scattered and torn,
Wish for the days when choices weren't worn.
Life took a turn, can't go back in time,
Grandparents' lessons, grateful for the climb.

(Verse 2)

Open doors with prayers for a better day,
Life breached, crossing borders, lost in disarray.
Where to turn, who to talk to, feeling alone,
Labelled as mental, disorder in every tone.

(Chorus)

How did we get here, destruction served on a plate,
Kids growing up, no choice, dictated fate.
Lost and confused, forced into a mould,
Let them be kids, let their stories unfold.

(Bridge)

Grown folks struggle, feet off the ground,
Power and greed, on the fringe they're bound.
Banks dictate, choosing who will rise or fall,
Daily lies we tell, just to stand tall.

(Verse 3)

Who's coming up? Or who's going down?
Life and death, a daily rundown.
Little white lies to get through the strife,
At the end of the day, what's left but life?

(Outro)

Peace to all, wish you a nice life,

In a world of chaos, navigating the strife.

I'm out, but the echoes remain,

In the hope that tomorrow breaks the chain.

WAGES POEM:

How come the wages are so low and the cost is so high?
Only for cooperate greed to align their pockets.
How come the locals are being outsourced being forced to live on the streets as the homeless population is on the streets.
Bruised and battered how come I didn't listen now, I'm scattered worn torn clothes that are tatter.
Where did my life take a left turn? wish I could go back to the days where I could have made better choices.
Where I was very happy. I'm blessed for my grandparents to teach me about God. Now I can pray for a better day with doors being open that God can open. My life has been breached where do I turn too?
Where do I go? Who do I talk too? With them thinking I'm mental or have some kind of disorder my life has crossed so many borders how come there is so much destruction with hate that is served to us on a plate?

As our kids are growing up, they can not even make a choice for themselves. Straight out of the gate everything we know love and cherish is gone and our kids are lost and confused, because everything is forced into their life's thinking that it's OK to be one way and not who you are born to be that you can change your body. Leave our children alone let them be kids with a childhood.
Grown folks are having trouble keeping their feet on the ground and food in the fridge because of power and greed is on the fringe of the banks. Who's coming? Who is going? What is going up? Who is coming down? Who chooses to live? Or who chooses to die? Each day as we live, we tell ourselves,

little white lies just to get by. At the end of the day what can you say or how can you pray? Peace have a nice life cause I'm out.

PLAYING THE FOOL:

(Verse 1)

I may seem nice, a facade I wear with pride,

But deep within, there's an asshole I can't hide.

Reached my limits, now I'm breaking free,

Unleashing rage that was bottled inside me.

(Chorus)

Ohh, don't you see, the struggle within me,

Life's chaos, choices, a painful decree.

Bleeding into dreams, as I lay down to sleep,

Life is cruel, playing the fool so deep.

(Verse 2)

In this endless fight, dragging weary feet,

Gathering scraps, trying to make life sweet.

How do I go on in this chaotic mess?

Talk is cheap, choices leave me in distress.

(Chorus)

Ohh, can't you feel, the weight that's so real,
Choices are painful, making wounds that won't heal.
Bleeding into dreams, as I lay down to sleep,
Life is cruel, playing the fool so deep.

(Bridge)

Trying to grasp, afraid to unmask,
Working hard, yet feeling so harassed.
Ashamed and defeated, goals seem far away,
Desires and dreams, at my feet, they lay.

(Chorus)

Ohh, don't you know, I'm trying to grow,
Life's bitter lessons, a relentless blow.
Bleeding into dreams, as I lay down to sleep,
Life is cruel, playing the fool so deep.

ENDLESS FIGHT:

I may look nice on the outside but I'm an asshole on the inside,

My limits have been reached and now I have been broken unleashing the rage that was built up,

So tired of this endless fight,

Draggin my feet barely standing up only to get a few scraps and bring it together.

How can I keep going on like this?

Life is chaos, talk is cheap, choices are painful and I bleed myself to sleep.

Life is cruel only to be playing the fool.

Trying to get a grasp but afraid to take off this mask.

Ohh ohh don't you know I'm trying, I'm working hard only to feel. ashamed and defeat what is to be accomplished.

How is it to be admonished? Desires and dreams laid at my feet.

BATTELING ADVERSITY:

There is always a battle to fight

Unexpected adversity to knock down

A hill to climb.

I've tried to talk to God but no answer, everything was still silent it has been deadly quiet.

The Devil is all around me with the demons that are in inside of me about to give in. That's when I fell on my knees talking to God seeking his presence, his grace in essence came to me live free my son in me, God showed up in ways, I never knew. The Devil tried to get me but God, wouldn't let me give in I'm living free despite of me.

I'm living free despite the devil trying to get at me.

In the battle of life, facing adversity's frown,

Climbing hills, seeking answers, feeling down.

Spoke to God, silence echoed, deadly quiet,

Demons within, devil's whispers incite.

Fell on my knees, seeking God's embrace,

His presence, grace, revealed in that sacred space.

"Live free, my son," His voice whispered true,
Defying the Devil, God's strength pulled me through. I'm living free despite of me I'm living free despite the devil trying to get at me.

TRADITIONAL LETTERS:

In the traditional style of letters, allow me to illustrate with an example. Let's embark on this introspective journey without the weight of tension. I find myself on a mission, unburdened by conditions. Dear God, there are myriad of questions weighing on my heart. How can parents be so destructive? Why do they shatter the hopes and dreams of their children to the point of extinguishing them? Grant me insight into this darkness.

I grapple with my past, aware that the solace of good days is fleeting. Despite attempts to pray and escape, exhaustion and frayed nerves prevail. Why did you allow the framework of life to be so abusive that my brother chose to end his own?

The world bewilders me. Why must hate persist? Why does religion turn into a perpetual debate? As a grown individual taught to procreate, is this my destined fate? Life feels like an upheaval from the start, a perpetual merry-go-round with no escape. Left with nothing but to stand up and shout, I release the emotions pent up inside. Dear God, why does hate persist? Temptation surrounds me like bait. Why must this world dismantle what you have created?

BEAUTY OF THE LAND:

The vast plains are open with the grass as tall as my knees with the wind blowing softly against my skin, through my hair, hearing the gushing sound blow past my ears, as the tree tips are green with a splendours mountain view as there are grey storm clouds in the sky with the roar of thunder as the sound crashes through the plains and echoes into the midst of the field. I stand still look up and take a deep breath as I breath it all in. I slowly look around and all's I see is the grim reaper of death with his black monk robe and his sickle. Roaming the plains hovering through the fields looking taking his time as he aims, waiting patiently I start to run, my heart pounding hard I'm not ready to go, am I dreaming? Is this real? I ask myself where am I? Am I between heaven and hell? I am so confused what is death after? What I keep asking myself, is my time up? I have so much to accomplish. Why is this happening? How did I get here?

STRIVING TO FIGHT:

(Verse 1)

In the shadows of my mind, I'm hurting, I'm trying,
Aching soul, can't tell how long I'll endure this ride.
Fallen far from grace, lost in the maze,
Longing for childhood times, those familiar faces.

(Pre-Chorus)

So much chaos, can't handle the load,
Sinking deep into a depression, on this heavy road.
Hard-pressed, can't carry on, can't ignore,
Running down the road, trying to outrun this inner war.

(Chorus)

Give me another day, just a little bit longer, little more time.
Sip from the bottle, trying to grow stronger.
Hold on tight, in this rock and roll, we sway,
Through the hurt and pain, find a better way.

(Verse 2)

Around the corner, I hide my strife,
A little drink to ease the storms of life.
Shoot up, drink up, run from the fall,
In the darkness, chasing echoes on this inner wall.

(Bridge)

Searching for solace in the neon light,
A symphony of chaos, a desperate flight.
But I need another day, a chance to find,
A melody of hope in this rhythm of the grind.

(Chorus)

Give me another day, just a little bit longer, a little more time
Sip from the bottle, trying to grow stronger.
Hold on tight, in this rock and roll, we sway, Through the hurt and pain, find a better way.

(Outro)

As the chords fade and the night grows dim,

I'll face tomorrow, find the strength within.

Through the highs and lows, the melody's call,

In the rock and roll, I'll rise, I won't fall.

JUST A BROKE FATHER:

I ain't got no money right now.

Bills are due but don't get paid til two weeks everything is always so tight.

Broke as hell I don't know what to do why is it always a fight.

Have no gas, no money, no money to buy food for the kids.

All's, I do is work ten days straight I barely lie down to even sleep with no days off while I work three jobs.

Ain't got plates to eat on, ain't got no more money for no gas, car shuts down not able to get another one. Credit score ain't shit. Always in the negative, I struggle to pull myself up.

When a bill comes up and gets paid here comes the other ones to help me get behind.

The Roaming Humbled man:

(Verse 1)

Once a hero soaring high, dreams painted in the sky,

Woke up, choices askew, my dreams unravelling too.

A hero turned to zero, but in losses, I found my hero.

(Chorus)

I was a hero, now a zero,

In the fight, I've found my true hero.

A journey through the cold and older,

In my losses, I became bolder.

(Verse 2)

No home, yet in the fight, I roamed,

For my kids, I gave my all, my love a steady tone.

Taught them well, from the heart I spoke,

Hoping my words linger when I'm broke.

(Chorus)

I was a hero, now a zero,
In the fight, I've found my true hero.
A journey through the cold and older,
In my losses, I became bolder.

(Bridge)

As I age, the story unfolds,
From a hero's tale to the chill, it holds.
Colder I've become, lessons unfold,
In the echoes of time, my story's told.

(Verse 3)

Fallen from grace, from hero to zero,
Yet, wisdom gained, like an aged hero.
With every step, as I grow colder,
I find strength in losses, my life's folder.

(Chorus)

I was a hero, now a zero,
In the fight, I've found my true hero.
A journey through the cold and older,
In my losses, I became bolder.

(Outro)

From hero to zero, my story's embrace,
In every stumble, a hero finds grace.
Through the ages, in life's colder,
I discover strength, as I grow older.

Poor hard-working Father: THE POEM:

I was a hero became zero,

I dreamed big, woke up on the wrong side, made my choices it all back fired on me that's when I realized that my losses made me.

I was hero who became a zero,

I have lived in this fight even when I didn't have a home. Did what I could for my kids. I hope I had taught them; hope that I had spoken well often from the heart. I pray they have heard me with my words. In part when I have fallen from being a hero who became a zero as I am aged, gotten older I have become colder.

Chapter 12

DRINK THE MEMORY AWAY:

I got high today cause I couldn't cope

I'm only living cause I know I'm dying.

That's why I smoke the dope because I've lost all of my hope.

I've got high today cause I can't deal with life on the day to day.

So, I made my room a haze of smoke

I'm hiding, I'm running away don't know what to do cause I have nothing left.

So, I light another toke.

I'm tired of the masses forming against me it always has to be something can't make it easy to live on easy street.

So, I got high today cause I couldn't cope so I got high today to live and I don't know how to obey, I couldn't be what I am not.

I am who I am;

So, I drink the memory away.

NO BOUNDARIES:

I have always been that person,

to push the boundaries.

While I have one foot off the ledge;

with one foot on the ground.

I'm leaning towards the edge more than on the ground,

all's it takes is one little push.

I have pushed till it breaks the heart, pounding with nothing surrounding me.

But I'm never satisfied, no matter how hard I have tried.

I just want to be isolated all the way around.

No one near but just myself and I; on my own.

When the rain is pouring how do you stay dry? Who is there to comfort you?

When the wind is blowing how do you stay in place am I'm being blown off the edge?

I have nothing to show so when the rain is pouring down on me where do I go?

WISHFUL PLEA:

I have tried, I hope they say yes
I pray for the best outcome.
But sometimes it is there to protect you.
Even when it's a disappointment in your eyes.
All’s I want to do is to make it better for you.
In earnest effort, I've sought a nod,
Hoping for a yes, invoking a hopeful God.
Prayers ascend for the best, a wishful plea,
Yet, sometimes, "no" guards, cold as can be.
Disappointment lingers in your gaze,
Yet, in the shadow, resilience stays.
All I aspire, in the quiet night's cue,
Is to mend and make it better for you.

VANQUISH THE FEAR:

(Verse 1)

Learned to be fearless, kept the fire alive in me,
Never let the flame extinguish, faced life's stormy sea.
Anguish was my companion, but now I stand strong,
Living on my own terms, where I truly belong.

(Chorus)

Vanquished the past, no sight or thought of you,
Dark memories linger, devil inside wants to play it through.
Outcast by society, always criticized, no one by my side,
Blame me for actions, judge the surface, let truth hide.

(Verse 2)

Broken home, nowhere to lay my head,
Left out in the cold, a nomad left unfed.
But I rise from the shadows, stronger than before,
Defying the odds, closing the pain's door.

(Chorus)

Vanquished the past, no sight or thought of you,
Dark memories linger, devil inside wants to play it through.
Outcast by society, always criticized, no one by my side,
Blame me for actions, judge the surface, let truth hide.

(Bridge)

I question; Why do you blame me? Why do you hate?
A journey from darkness, breaking through fate.

The devil inside wants to play, but I stand tall,
Overcoming struggles, rising from the fall.

(Verse 3)

No longer haunted by the echoes of despair,
I break free from the chains, breathe in the fresh air.
The world may have rejected me, but I won't conform,
For in being myself, I weathered the storm.

(Chorus)

Vanquished the past, no sight or thought of you,
Dark memories linger, Devil inside wants to play it through.
Outcast by society, always criticized, no one by my side,
Blame me for actions, judge the surface, let truth hide.

(Outro)

So, as I move forward, leaving the pain behind,
I find strength in resilience, a new narrative to bind.
The Devil may whisper, memories may stay,
But I am the author, shaping a new day.

JUST PLAIN SURVIVING:

(Verse 1)

I was born to survive, destined to fight,
In the battleground of life, under the moonlight.
A warrior's spirit, never giving up the fight,
In the midst of it all, I'll stand tall with all my might.

(Chorus)

I put my heart and soul into every stride,
Living free, breaking free from the ties that bind.
Born to fight, born to survive,
I'll keep pushing forward, never looking behind.

(Verse 2)

Through the trials and the pain, I've seen it all,
Heard words that cut deep, like a relentless squall.
But I won't be swayed by the lies that surround,
I'm breaking free, departing from what once was bound.

(Chorus)

I put my heart and soul into every stride,
Living free, breaking free from the ties that bind.
Born to fight, born to survive,
I'll keep pushing forward, never looking behind.

(Bridge)

In the shadows, I've moulded the man I've become,
Yet you don't know me, it's like I'm on the run.
I'll rise above, standing tall and free,
The man I am, forever evolving, you'll never see.

(Chorus)

I put my heart and soul into every stride,
Living free, breaking free from the ties that bind.
Born to fight, born to survive,
I'll keep pushing forward, never looking behind.

(Outro)

So here I am, a warrior strong and true,

No longer held back, breaking through.

I've discovered myself, now it's time to be,

The person I am, forever wild and free.

SPIRITUAL SOUL:

We all have a spirit we all have a soul,

We all live and breathe.

With hearts pumping and blood flowing,

We love and We hate!

We are vulnerable but we also come together.

We try not to put over on anyone but at times we feel jealous of others.

The strength that is in us, tells us to push on, to keep moving forward it's the drive of not giving up no matter how hard it gets. No matter how rich or poor we are. It's the humanity that gives us life so never give up, keep putting one foot in front of the other continue to evolve. Let's get problems solved, let's continue to live not only for ourselves but for others as well. Kindness and love are what everyone could use.

That's a beautiful sentiment. Kindness and love can truly make a difference in our lives and in the lives of others. It's important to remember that we are all connected and that by showing compassion and understanding, we can create a more harmonious world. Let's continue to support each other, uplift one another, and work together to overcome challenges and make a positive impact.

LONGING FOR CRUELTY:

I'm longing for change for myself but I don't know how. My life has been so hard-core not much more, so much abandonment. Was I so containment that I couldn't be loved, held, or hugged?

So much abuse I guess it gave my parents an excuse, always had to learn the hard way on my own I've tried to hide I've tried to surrender but I feel so lost.

I'm longing for a change for myself but I can't do it by myself life has been cruel. Everywhere I have been Anywhere I have grown I have been hated. I don't want stay here.

I want to feel loved,
Want to know I belong.
Just want to cut loose.
I have just to be me
Want my heart beat to make a mark before I leave.
I'm ready to let go and be at peace.

I'm ready to tell my truth where you can't escape. It won't be hard to see.
I'm not giving up even though life has wanted me to be dead.
Lie awake at night wishing I could make a song I know I am not strong but forgive me as I don't follow along with the crowd.
This is my mind.
I wish I had a voice to be heard wish I had vocals to turn heads but here are my words.

(Verse 1)
Everywhere I roam, faced hate in my zone,
Grew up feeling alone, now I'm ready to be known.
Not gonna stay stuck, need that love, no more tough luck,
Just wanna belong, cut loose, let my spirit erupt.

(Chorus)
Feel the rhythm in my beat, making marks on the street,
Burning to be free, leaving a legacy, no defeat.
Ready to find peace, share my truth, never cease,

Break the chains, my voice released, making noise that won't decrease.

(Verse 2)
I've been ready to let go, tell my tale, let it flow,
In a world where I grow, where my authenticity shows.
Life tried to bring me down, make me wear a crown,
But I won't give up, won't let the darkness drown.

(Bridge)
Late nights, I lie awake, dreams I wanna make,
Crafting a song, proving I'm not fake.
Not the strongest, but won't conform,
In the crowd, I stand apart, weathering the storm.

(Chorus)
Feel the rhythm in my beat, making marks on the street,
Burning to be free, leaving a legacy, no defeat.
Ready to find peace, share my truth, never cease,

Break the chains, my voice released, making noise that won't decrease.

(Outro)
This is my mind, my voice to be heard,
Wishing for vocals that turn heads undisturbed.
I won't give in, won't be misled,
In the symphony of life, my song will spread.

MELODY FOR A STORY TO UNFOLD:

(Verse 1)

In the rhythm of life, where music takes its toll,
A melody of the soul, a story to unfold.
I dance to a drum, a beat uniquely spun,
A tale of my journey, until the setting sun.

(Chorus)

If fate should intervene and take me away,
Promise me, dear friend, my legacy will stay.
Keep making the music, let it soar and fly,
To new heights and lengths, reaching the sky.

(Verse 2)

Life's a canvas, paint it with your might,
Take the road less travelled, into the night.
Growth is the mantra, wisdom your guide,
Never pause, never halt, let the stars be your pride.

(Chorus)

If ever I'm gone, let the notes carry on,
Echo through time, like the breaking dawn.
Keep making the music, let it soar and fly,
To new heights and lengths, reaching the sky.

(Bridge)

Don't fear the unknown, embrace the chase,
In every setback, find a new grace.
The symphony of life, play it with glee,
A legacy of music, forever set free.

(Verse 3)

Strive for brilliance, let your spirit ignite,
Forge ahead, illuminate the darkest night.
Keep evolving, keep learning, never stand still,
A perpetual crescendo, an unyielding thrill.

(Chorus)

If I'm but a memory, let the music speak,
Through each note, in the strong and the meek.
Keep making the music, let it soar and fly,
To new heights and lengths, reaching the sky.

(Outro)

So, dance to your rhythm, and let it be known,
In the heartbeat of music, seeds of greatness are sown.
If I'm not here, let the melody persist,
A testament to life, in each passionate twist.

LIFE HAS FADED AWAY:

I'm slipping away in my own mind
As the day fades away.
Everything in my life has faded away
Left alone lost and confused.
How can I let things go so I can move on?
Don't know how to unwind even if the sun comes up tomorrow.
I feel the snake bite as the venom runs through my blood.
I lay there in the night.

BLEEDING:

[Verse 1]

I'm bleedin', I'm bleedin,' can't you see me?

My heart's cryin' out, won't you set me free?

[Chorus]

Oh, heaven please come and rescue me,

All I got left is my soul to plead.

[Verse 2]

Let me be free of this pain and misery,

Ohh, please let me free of this pain and misery.

[Verse 3]

In the darkness, I've been lost for so long,

Searching for a place where I belong.

I've faced the storms, the battles, and the strife,

But still, I hold on to this fragile life.

[Verse 4]
With every scar, I've learned to grow,
Through the tears and pain, I’ve come to know.
Life's a journey, filled with twists and turns,
But in my heart, a flicker of hope still burns.

[Verse 5]
Through the shadows, I've walked
this lonely road,
Carrying burdens, a heavy, crushing load.
But I won't surrender, I won't give in,
I'll keep on fighting, searching for a win.

[Verse 6]
As the night falls, and the stars softly gleam,
I'll hold on tighter to my shattered dream.
With each sunrise, I’ll find the strength to rise,
In the face of despair, I'll reach for the skies.

WORLD OF ILLUSION:

(Verse 1)

In this mentally ill life, a chaotic ride,

No medication soothes, emotions collide.

No chill, everything's out of hand,

World spinning, taken a step, can't understand. No one's listening, heart pounding loud,

Untreated, lost in society's crowd.

Expected to thrive, but I feel defeated,

Go crazy, society's blame is repeated.

(Chorus)

On the warpath, wondering why I'm alive,

Soul crying, intentions to set the world on fire.

No denial, lost in a world of illusion,

Mentally ill, facing society's confusion.

(Verse 2)

Eyes gleaming with nothing but lies,

Where does the mentally ill find their ties?

Washed down, thrown away, signs ignored,
No job, no pay, abandoned, adored.
Alone in a world with no one to care,
Acting out, astray, with loneliness to bear.
Who to turn to, who to cry out to,
Surrounded by solitude, what more to pursue?

(Chorus)
On the warpath, wondering why I'm alive, Soul crying,
intentions to set the world on fire.
No denial, lost in a world of illusion,
Mentally ill, facing society's confusion.

(Bridge)
Acting out, lost in my mind,
Already lost, what more to find?
Stranded, abandoned, no one nearby,
Loneliness surrounds, drowning in fear.

(Verse 3)

No care from anyone, come and get me,
What more to lose when already set free?
In my mind's chaos, acting out alone,
Society's judgment, a heart turned to stone.

(Chorus)

On the warpath, wondering why I'm alive,
Soul crying, intentions to set the world on fire.
No denial, lost in a world of illusion,
Mentally ill, facing society's confusion.

(Outro)

In the silence, echoes of loneliness persist,
Searching for solace, in a world that's dismissed.
But still, I stand, resilient and strong,
Hoping someday, I'll find where I belong.

RISING ASHES FROM LIFE:

(Verse 1)

Depression ain't my master, won't let it take control,

Rising from the ashes, mending this wounded soul.

Dare I face the day, put on my worn-out dress clothes on,

In this admission of struggle, I find strength to confess.

(Chorus)

Every day's a battle, but I'll keep on goin',

Anger at the helm, my emotions overflowin'.

Put on my boots, walkin' down the line,

Staring at the Devil, sayin' "Not today, not this time."

(Verse 2)

Fightin' through the darkness, ain't no easy climb,

But I won't let the shadows steal away my prime.

Rooted in my journey, I lace up my pride,

Walking through the fire, with determination as my guide.

(Chorus)

Every day's a challenge, can't let it break me,
Anger may linger, but hope is what I'll see.
Boots on my feet, keepin' steady in the grind,
Facing every demon, leaving them behind.

(Bridge)

In the fine eye of the Devil, I take my stand, Not today,
not tomorrow, not as long as I can. Mind heavy with
burdens, but I won’t resign,
I’ll keep on walkin one step at a time.

(Chorus)

Won’t surrender to the darkness, won’t give in,
Anger may echo, but it’s hope that’ll win. Broken but
unyielding, in this uphill climb,
With my boots on, I’ll keep walkin’ down the line.

TRUE BELIEVE:

True belief lies in the spirit of your heart.

Your soul carries you through faith

What lies is what may.

Dream is a direction of what one will follow one who believes one who desires.

Yes, you will fall, yes you will fail.

But your strength is what will carry you through with your faith to hold you up right.

It doesn't matter where you are going or how steep the dream is, it all begins with one step of faith come what may in this day.

The pleasures of life are the entertainment to heal out the pain of one's life, to laugh, to cry, to feel pain, to heal.

The pestilence is one who destroys the soul but with faith we live on.

LIFE'S LESSONS

(Verse 1)

Come my way, through the hard days,
No easy street or byways, just the hard way,
Learning life's lessons, day by day,
In this rough life, got a lot to say.

(Chorus)

Had to learn the hard way, to live my life,
In the struggle and the strife,
When life's not fair, don't despair,
Keep moving on, show you care.

(Verse 2)

Give your all, but time won't repay,
Keep pushing forward, come what may,
In this crazy world, with crazy lives,
Still, keep on moving, as the road unwinds.

(Chorus)

Had to learn the hard way, to live my life,
In the struggle and the strife,
When life's not fair, don't despair,
Keep moving on, show you care.

(Bridge)

Don't quit, don't give up, it'll be okay,
Sit down, have a beer, or a drink, they say, In this crazy world, with its twists and turns, Keep on moving, as the fire burns.

(Verse 3)

Through the highs and lows, and the twists of fate,
Life's a journey, not a fixed state,
Give it your all, with a heart so true,
Even when life doesn't do right by you.

(Chorus)

Had to learn the hard way, to live my life,
In the struggle and the strife,
When life's not fair, don't despair,
Keep moving on, show you care.

(Outro)

So, keep on moving, down the road,
With every step, let your story unfold,
In this crazy world, with its highs and lows,
You've still got to keep on, as the river flows.

MENTALLY ILL:

Mentally ill life get so crazy no medication helps, emotions have no chill everything out of hand my world spinning taken one step not even winning no one listening.

My heart pounding,

Go untreated lost into society, expected to thrive but I feel defeated, I go crazy but then society blames you, judges you, with no care for you, that's when the war path starts.

I still wonder why I'm alive!

Even when my soul cries I don't deny my ill forgotten intentions to set the world on fire.

With out care I don't dare deny it.

Nothing is as it seems while the look in the eye gleams with nothing but lies. Where does the mentally ill go?

Washed down thrown away.

Get ignored all the signs missed no job, no pay, stranded, abandoned alone with not a fucking care from anyone.

Come and get me. What more do I have to lose? When I have already lost in my mind. Acting out, acting astray, with not a soul nearby. Who to turn too? Who to cry out too? Why am I always surrounded by loneliness? I'm here but no one to care. Just know life with in it’s self is not fair.

DISAPPEAR TO LET MY DEMONS PLAY:

What would happen if I were disappear? Tired of living this life in full of fear.

All's, I have ever gotten good at in life is to be fired.

There is something that ain't right in me. Why am I wired the wrong way?

Would my family be lost in the gate ways of life?

After everything I have done, I have tried to do right, just oh so tired of doing that right thing while losing at the same time.

I walk on the ground while it's a landmine.

Wish I could turn back the time to be at peace in these rugged times.

Work hard to provide for my family barely paying the bills but yet. Some how, some way, I'm the bad guy, I'm the one who is blamed for everything.

They lied to me, they shut me out.

What better way is there when the monsters are out to kill you.

That's when your demons take over to protect you, I let my demons free is dangerous for you. I know that I know I am free I'm not mistaken cause there ain't no way back.

FIGHT BEFORE YOU LOSE YOUR MIGHT:

In this fight in the burrow of struggle where defeat is at your feet.

Hold strong take courage cause the light is on for you.

Don't give up, don't give in even if you lose all of your might. All's you have to do is to keep fighting through the night as the light is on for you.

Know I'll be here for you!

A shoulder to cry on you no longer have to swim in this pond of confusion.

Know I'll be here for you with the light on!

Don't give up, Don't give in, keep fighting through the night cause the light is on here for you.

MEMORIES IN LIVING VESSEL:

What lies in the mystery of the memory? What cries from the mind of tragedy?

What comes from a horrific nightmare that became real?

How does one as in so much to feel?

What is in the depths of the crushed heart?

It's hard to feel when your heart is in Fear.

In my own mind working trying to switch gears.

But thoughts screaming in my head.

Dreaming of what could be dead.

Living in this vessel not knowing what is next.

What cries, what lies, in my darkness that is run deep in my memories. Come get me, cause I’m done, I'm gone, no more to tell the only way I can express is to yell in my own hell.

ENIGMA OF LIFE:

In the realm where shadows dance, the meaning of death,
A mystic query, a whispered breath.
Life's enigma, a tale untold,
In the fabric of existence, mysteries unfold. The heart of Man, a compass true, Guiding us through the foggy hue. Amidst the clamour, a silent plea, Do we strive to set each other free?
Yet, voices lost, unnoticed cries,
In the echo chamber where silence lies. Through the cracks, many souls slip, In the cacophony, their presence a cryptic grip. Violence echoes, drowning the serene, Erasing footprints, where hypocrisy convenes. Beneath the deceit, let truth lay bare, As we ponder if peace awaits us there. Did we do enough, did we persist? In the tapestry of life, does our thread resist? For those who mourn, let truth unfold, Let hearts be seen, let stories be told. A message whispered, a plea sincere, May wise hearts listen, may deaf ears clear.

Hysterical ride:

(Verse 1)

Woke up this morning, job uncertainty in the air,
Not sure if it's a good day or burdened with despair.
Turn the knob to face the world, caught in pouring rain,
Lost in the storm, uncertain which path to gain.

(Chorus)

Bills piling up, mortgage overdue,
Feeling blue, seeking a miracle, it's true.
Life's a hysterical ride, a miracle I'm here,
Holding on, but at times, gotta let go, persevere.

(Verse 2)

Juggling decisions, each step a puzzle piece,
Life's a struggle, longing for release.
My world's crumbling, uncertainties abound,
Who remains, what stays, who's with me, yet to be found.

(Bridge)
In this chaos, I hold my ground,
Even when it feels like life's unwound.
Stand by myself, fake ones by my side,
Discovering strength, on this unpredictable ride.

(Chorus)
Bills piling up, mortgage overdue,
Feeling blue, seeking a miracle, it's true.
Life's a hysterical ride, a miracle I'm here,
Holding on, but at times, gotta let go, persevere.

(Verse 3)
Every decision, just a piece in the juggle,
As I navigate a life that continues to bubble.
Letting go at times, to truly live,
Embracing the uncertainty, it's all we can give.

(Outro)

So, I’ll face the storms, let the crumbles fall,
In the chaos, find strength, stand tall.
Who remains, what stays, time will unveil,
In this journey of life, resilience will prevail

Smile in Silence:

(Verse 1)

In the moonlight, I ride so light,

Chasing pills, seeking thrills, with Seether in the night.

Aggressive violator, dancing on the edge,

Nurse user, juggling life's unpredictable pledge.

(Pre-Chorus)

Job undone, interrupted by the setting sun,

Wishing for a trigger, just to make it all undone.

(Chorus)

Surprises unfold, asking why it's no fun,

Dreaming of a jackpot, wanting to be the chosen one.

Mental agony, nerves on the fringe,

Smiling on the outside, while inside I cringe.

(Verse 2)

A narcotics binge, chasing the thrill,
Pills and whisky, a dangerous fill.
Feeling the chills, as the night unfolds,
In this twisted tale, where the darkness moulds.

(Bridge)

Capacity on the fringe, nerves on alert,
Stabbed in the back, anger starts to assert.
Fake admiralty, put on a smile,
No cavalry in sight, just a lonely mile.

(Chorus)

Surprises unfold, asking why it's no fun,
Dreaming of a jackpot, wanting to be the chosen one.
Mental agony, nerves on the fringe,
Smiling on the outside, while inside I cringe.

(Outro)

In the silence, echoes of a troubled mind,
Seeking solace, a way to leave it all behind.
Light rider, pain pill seeker, in this darkened den,
Hoping for a dawn, when the night will end.

Melody for a story to unfold:

(Verse 1)

In the rhythm of life, where music takes its toll,
A melody of the soul, a story to unfold.
I dance to a drum, a beat uniquely spun,
A tale of my journey, until the setting sun.

(Chorus)

If fate should intervene and take me away,
Promise me, dear friend, my legacy will stay.
Keep making the music, let it soar and fly,
To new heights and lengths, reaching the sky.

(Verse 2)

Life's a canvas, paint it with your might,
Take the road less travelled, into the night.
Growth is the mantra, wisdom your guide,
Never pause, never halt, let the stars be your pride.

(Chorus)

If ever I'm gone, let the notes carry on,
Echo through time, like the breaking dawn.
Keep making the music, let it soar and fly,
To new heights and lengths, reaching the sky.

(Bridge)

Don't fear the unknown, embrace the chase,
In every setback, find a new grace.
The symphony of life, play it with glee,
A legacy of music, forever set free.

(Verse 3)

Strive for brilliance, let your spirit ignite,
Forge ahead, illuminate the darkest night.
Keep evolving, keep learning, never stand still,
A perpetual crescendo, an unyielding thrill.

(Chorus)

If I'm but a memory, let the music speak,
Through each note, in the strong and the meek.
Keep making the music, let it soar and fly,
To new heights and lengths, reaching the sky.

(Outro)

So, dance to your rhythm, and let it be known,
In the heartbeat of music, seeds of greatness are sown.
If I'm not here, let the melody persist,
A testament to life, in each passionate twist.

GET A GRIP:

Rip rip drip drip I can't even a get a grip grip on this life of mine I'm drowning in my own punishment feeling being shot from gunshot everything around me is turning into a plot. Give up give in the strength that is in me is not there now it's been taken with a ripped heart].

The darkness is the only friend I have here is what is in my thoughts along with my body on this journey by myself on my own this time being lonely and missing you. I have crossed the line and there is no turning back. Poison is in my blood fighting the demons that has been a waste of time, because of defeat with the crushing blow of death finally took me. I've been shunned in been shut out travelled down the road only to be ignored I said the hell with it put my foot down on the ground only to get up now. Life goes on and gets so heavy, so much insanity all around me is calamity this life has treaded on me wanna be invisible but I am being pulled like a racehorse my body dragged through the dirt and mud I finally collapse so

calloused and coarse all over so take me away burn me up cut me loose and let me go cause I'm never good enough. I thought I was tough only to realize that I am weak.
Drip drip I can't even get a grip on this life of mine.
Drowning in my own punishment feeling being shot from a gunshot given up given in the strength that is in me is not there now it's been taken with a ripped heart.

Made in the USA
Las Vegas, NV
28 November 2024

689d624e-cf49-4bd8-97fa-002ef71e5888R01